The
Leisure
Pen

The Leisure Pen

A Book For Elderwriters

By **Joyce S. Steward**
and **Mary K. Croft**

Library of Congress Catalog Card Number: 88-82602

Main entry under title:

The Leisure Pen.

ISBN 0-9621354-0-2

Keepsake Publishers
P.O. Box 21
Plover, Wisconsin 54467

Acknowledgments

CHAPTER 1

From *Enjoy Old Age: A Program of Self-Management* by B. F. Skinner and M. E. Vaughan. Copyright © 1983. Reprinted by permission of W. W. Norton and Company, Inc.
Excerpt from "To Rest Is To Rust" by Helen Hayes. Reprinted with permission of United Press International, Copyright © 1985.
Excerpts from *What My Heart Wants to Tell* by Verna Mae Slone. Reprinted with permission of New Republic Books.

CHAPTER 2

From WRITER'S ART by James J. Kilpatrick. Copyright © 1984 UNIVERSAL PRESS SYNDICATE. Reprinted with permission. All rights reserved.
Lines of "Advice" and "On His Magic Box" by Leo Rosten. Both reprinted by permission of the author.
From "A Letter to John T. Bartlett, 22 February 1914," by Robert Frost. *Selected Letters of Robert Frost*, edited by Lawrance Thompson. Copyright © 1964 Holt, Rinehart and Winston, Inc. Reprinted by permission.
From JOURNAL OF A NOVEL: THE EAST OF EDEN LETTERS by John Steinbeck. Copyright © 1969 by the Executors of the Estate of John Steinbeck. All rights reserved. Reprinted by permission of Viking Penguin, Inc.

All other literary credits appear on pages 203-206, which constitute a legal extension of the copyright page.

Contents

Part I

Writing
and
You

Chapter 1

Why Write?

$\mathcal{A}$bout the time you pick up a free admission pass to the National Parks or ask for a ten-percent savings card at the fast food outlet, you probably realize that library shelves and current magazines now aim countless books and articles at "the senior reader"—advice on keeping healthy, retiring happily, managing your money, remaining alert in the changing world. The publishers know there are a lot of us over fifty—and they are reaching out to us. Even Dr. Seuss, who used to write exclusively for your grandchildren, got into the act recently with his book *You're Only Old Once!*

Just as you see all this writing aimed at you, you'll also discover more and more people who are finding time to write now that they've finished some other career. Helen Hooven Santmyer published *And Ladies of the Club*, a first novel, when she was in her late eighties. Harriet Doerr suddenly "found fame" with her *Stones for Ibarra* when she was seventy-four. Norman Maclean retired and then wrote his autobiographical book on fishing, *A River Runs Through It.*

Writing knows no age limits. As Dr. Johnson said two hundred years ago, "A man may write at any time if he sets himself doggedly to it." Now even though he probably wasn't thinking about writing at any age, his point is that what you need in order to write is simply to want to!

Why should you, though? Most of us may not find an audience of eager readers or produce anything like a best seller, but there are a lot of good reasons for writing, even if you've never done much of it before. For one thing, psychologists tell us it is healthy—therapeutic.

In their book entitled *Enjoy Old Age: A Program of Self-Management*, B. F. Skinner and M. E. Vaughan say writing is a good way to keep in touch with the world and with the past. They advise writing in pocket notebooks, keeping records, jotting sentences that pin thoughts down and "keep them around to be used in subsequent thinking." They offer a slogan: "In place of memories, memoranda."

Helen Hayes, who is just as magnificent now as she was in the 1930's, gave this advice in an article called "To Rest Is To Rust."

> *I also like to see older folks write an "autobiography." Writing is very therapeutic. In fact, experts say it promotes self-esteem and personal integration. Personally, I think it also clears away the cobwebs and stimulates a fresh way of thinking and looking back on your life. Most important, perhaps, it leaves a private history of yourself and your family. Don't you wish your grandmother and her grandmother before her had done that?*

In the preface of *What My Heart Wants to Tell*, an autobiographical story of life in a small Kentucky town, Verna Mae Slone explains her reasons for writing.

> *Dear Grandchildren:*
> *I am writing you this letter to be read later when you are older and can understand.*
> *If you are the kind of folks who honor money and prestige, then I have very little to leave you: just*

*a few handmade quilts and a few old silver coins,
made and collected over my sixty years of life—not
much to show for a lifetime of hard work. But I hope
by writing this book, I can pass on to you the
heritage my father left me.*

*Materialwise, he only gave me an acre of land,
half of a house (the other half had been torn down),
a few handmade chairs, a basket, and less than two
hundred dollars in money. But believe me, I would
not exchange the memories I have of him for all the
gold in Fort Knox. And the truths and wisdom of life
he taught me have been a staff and a rod to comfort
me all the days of my life.*

*In this book I will try to pass on to you all my
memories of him.*

Those are good reasons even if you've never been a writer
before. Later on Verna Mae says,

*I guess my scribblings are like my crazy quilts,
without any form or unity. The more I write, the
more I remember. There are just so many things I
want to say, maybe some are interesting only to
me. Our young folks have lost so much without ever
knowing they had it to lose.*

You, too, may feel that your life isn't very spectacular, but
you have something to tell. And you can answer the question
"Why write?" in the same way Verna Mae does:

First, she writes for others—for the generations who come
after her.

Second, she writes for herself. She may discover this purpose only as she writes, for in the act of writing, she remembers more. She finds more things she wants to say. Even if she
doesn't put them into final form, they are creative in the way
her crazy quilts are—they are the patchwork of her life.

Those are very important reasons for writing as you grow older.

- to preserve and pass along thoughts and memories, the life you know, the way things were or are for you
- to recall and clarify, sort out and give order to things for yourself

Writing things down both gives them permanence and makes them clearer. Words are like the pictures we take to preserve the way someone looked, what it was like then, how a day was spent. We write on the back of the snapshot—date, background, people—lest we forget, even though we have the picture.

Verna Mae Slone's metaphor fits again: by "piecing" together your pattern of life, you have something "handmade" to pass along; and by sorting over memories and giving them form in writing, you make all your experiences a little less "crazy."

Benjamin Franklin, as he wrote his autobiography, said it this way: "The next thing most like living one's Life over again, seems to be a *Recollection* of that Life, and to make that Recollection as durable as possible, the putting it down in Writing."

Seniors Talk About Why They Write

Here are the reasons some of the seniors in our writing groups have given for starting to write.

Chris talks about why he started writing: "*I was always interested in history. You know, I taught it for awhile before I went into school administration. More and more I've thought about how the time in which we live affects people, how it shapes us and*

To understand
the past

makes us act the way we do. For instance, my generation is always worried about money. We often can't bring ourselves to spend, even if we have enough. 'Isn't that too high?' we ask. Or 'Isn't that foolish?' Our children accuse us of being tight, and we are, perhaps because of when we grew up. And I've thought about why those of us who were in the second World War had a hard time swallowing the trouble at the time of Vietnam. I wanted to get some of my ideas on paper, so the first year I retired and had time, I enrolled in an extension class at the community college. It has been great—I feel I'm getting my interpretations of history on paper.

To capture
memories

Eva told us, *"I read about this woman in the newspaper—our weekly gossip sheet, you know. She was having a hundredth birthday, with a big celebration at the senior center. We all went, even if we didn't know her real well. Well, they asked her to talk a bit and she was real alert. She told all about things she remembered—that movies used to cost ten cents in her town, for instance. Well, I told my grandson (who pays $4.00 to see a movie) about it, and told him we didn't have movies at all close to the ranch where I grew up. He couldn't believe all of it, and we started talking about other things and he said why didn't I write about what it was like where I grew up. He didn't know anything about my life really—how far we were from town, milking cows, cutting our wood, all that. I started writing some of it down—and it's been great remembering, even if no one ever reads it.*

Hank told us that he got stirred up about a park project in his town. *"I'd never written a letter to an editor before, not in all my seventy-two years. But when they decided*

To convince
others

to cut up that ravine where we used to hide out on Halloween, or go wading in the rush of the creek after spring flood—well, I was just angry and I let loose and wrote a hot one. Everyone started saying, 'Hank, you told 'em. Do it some more.' So I got to be a kind of speaker for several things some of us want around this community. Now I'm working on an ecology newsletter and spreading my objections—and some praise as well—around outside just this one town."

Frances has always been in love with words, and she said, *"I had to make a living when I was young and didn't get to finish college. I always knew I liked to write, to*

To share
the joy
of living

play with words and try to create a poem like some of them I read as a girl. I like the music and the pictures—the Psalms have always given me comfort. So every once in a while I'd write a little verse for some occasion—the stanzas we put in the front of the church cookbook, for instance, or a few lines for a birthday card I made. Now lately I've had more time. And as I sat watching the birds at the feeder one day, I decided to try to put what I saw into some poems— they aren't very good maybe, but they are mine, and other people seem to like them. I've written a series around the birds that come at different times and another about the garden at different seasons. Just little bits of nature's bounty—my own small way of saying I love things—of showing that they are beautiful."

To find an outlet—to heal the self

Marilyn mentioned that she had felt very lonely since her sister died, but *"now I'm snapping out of it. I'm the only one of my brothers and sisters left, and I was a little depressed. Even though my sister had been sick, I couldn't accept things. I began, on someone's suggestion, to write out my feelings. It really helped. Then I'd imagine that we were young again and I began to write about the happy times, too. I appreciate the wonderful years we had and it was healing to remember that. I told my doctor and he concurred. 'Much better than sleeping pills! Keep it up,' he said. I always liked reading the journals of famous people—especially those of writers—and even though the writing is primarily an outlet, I'm beginning to sound quite professional on paper."*

And Your Reasons?

You probably have reasons similar to some of these. Think about them, talk about them, write about them.

Chapter 2

Developing as a Writer

The act of writing is putting yourself on the line. This is where you proclaim "Hey, world. This is me." Here you celebrate yourself, even find yourself.

So what's the first step, you ask. The best advice we know comes from a famous French writer, Guy de Maupassant: "Get black on white." In other words—write. Get it down. Even if you think it's bad at first, it's the only way you can finally do anything good.

The old adage is true—you learn to write by writing. So here are some activities to get you started—whether alone, or in an informal group, or in an organized class.

Writing Places

Decide on a spot, a specific area where you will write. Create a writer's nest—a corner of a room with a view of an old oak tree, the room daughter Linda vacated when she was married, a portion of the rec room, even the laundry room— wherever you can build an inviting, comfortable environment. Make it yours—your writing place.

Indulge your eccentricities. Most writers do. Virginia Woolf had to have a table just the right height; Thomas Wolfe, over six feet tall, was comfortable using the top of a refrigerator as a desk. Robert Frost preferred a writing board. Robin Moore likes to write standing up, and he feeds a 200 foot roll of paper into his typewriter so he won't have to worry about coming to the end of a page!

Writing Tools

Once you have selected your "write place," equip it to suit your needs, your writing habits, even your fancy. Visit an office supply store and select the tools and paper just right for you. Some of us can write only if we have a legal pad and six, freshly sharpened #2.5 Mongol pencils. Others want a medium-point ballpoint pen. Others, Jacqueline Susann was one, prefer different colored paper for different drafts.

Leo Rosten claims, "There is no substitute for sitting down with a pen and pencil—not a typewriter—and putting something on paper every day." Certainly most of us would agree on the need for daily writing, but many would balk at his insistence on pen or pencil. You may prefer a mechanical aid—a trusty old Royal typewriter that hunt-and-pecked you through term papers perhaps. Or you might try a cassette recorder and first speak your thoughts and then copy them later.

Some of you—and this is another challenge—will enter the age of automation and equip yourselves with an electronic typewriter or word processor. Wonder of wonders! These mechanical aids not only make the physical act of writing easier, but they diminish the worry over neatness and correctness. Because you see your writing in a "printlike" form, it's easier to get on with the job of editing. Word processors make revision easier because they allow the writing to be maneuvered—words replaced, whole paragraphs moved about or added, as well as surface errors and misspellings to be corrected without messing up the page!

Know thy computer, though. Don't let ease of putting material on the screen and into your copy let you lapse into wordiness. Use the "delete" button to remove excesses as well as to make changes. Always remember that whatever your writing tools and habits, there is no such thing as good writing. There is only good rewriting.

Writing Ways

Important as finding or creating that working atmosphere is to your development as a writer, even more important are the resources within yourself—the memories, observations, and connections that bring forth ideas and provide the details that carry those ideas to your reader. Columnist-reviewer James J. Kilpatrick, who often writes wittily about language, has this to say about something every writer needs:

> Every good writer has a lumberyard. It is an area in our memory where we store images, impressions, similes, metaphors, lines of potential dialogue. We put them quietly away on the rafters. When the time comes to fashion a particular sentence, there they are.

Instead of a lumberyard, Leo Rosten recommends a magic box like his:

> This is a box someone gave me for Christmas years ago. It contained, originally, fruit, dates, and candy. I like that box. It is a good, stout cardboard box. It has dignity. It did its work well. I couldn't bring myself to throw it away. Instead, I fell into the habit of tossing into it notes I'd made, letters, clippings, ideas.

On a plane, say, I'd scribble notes on the back of an envelope. Then at home I'd throw them into that box. In would go a letter someone had sent me, a phrase I liked, a reminder to write a story about somebody who stole a book when he was ten. And now, every so often, I reach in and pick out a handful of notes and write a page from them.

The last page I did from my Magic Box contained about nine different items. One, the boo-boo of the year from the Boston Globe: *"All in all, this book fills a much needed void." An epigram from Chesterton on the woman's suffrage movement: "Twenty million English women arose with a cry—'we will not be dictated to'—and became stenographers . . . ."*

Your "Magic Box" can be a drawer, a folder, a large envelope . . . just so you have a place to keep your notes. Mark different things—epigrams, a tidbit of history, some remnant of biography. Pretty soon the notes begin to fall into categories. When you want something to write about, put your hands on something you've tucked away in your own "magic box."

With your treasury, your bank account always ready for deposits and withdrawals, you are ready to write. Just how you proceed is always personal, but here are some suggestions of little things that work . . . some of the time . . . for some of us:

Schedule a writing appointment with yourself to write daily, perhaps for only fifteen minutes. Start off by muttering, if you wish, internally or aloud, then writing—whatever comes to mind. Just write. About your feelings, your plans, your thoughts, even your inability to get started writing. Don't censor yourself. Reason and order are not a necessity at this stage. In fact, they will inhibit your freedom and free association. *Just write.*

Use old or cheap paper for these scribblings. This is not only economical and ecological, it is a way of reminding yourself that the writing is transient, not a final product.

Talk yourself into writing. There are times for all of us when the physical act of writing seems burdensome and inhibiting. In those moments you can sometimes get started by using a cassette recorder. The natural act of talking can be an easy entry into writing. Speak your thoughts about yourself, your day, your plans. Later transcribe your efforts or have someone do it for you. Talk often gets you on your way.

Give your ideas a tentative form. You are incensed over the transactions of the neighborhood dogs, and you want to say so in a letter to the editor. Or you want to express annoyance with television giveaway shows. Jot down the ideas you'd like to include. Or just write a trial draft. Such tentative writing helps you discover what you want to say and what you don't, what works and what doesn't. And the first draft helps vent feelings before you go on to write the more reasoned and appropriate—and more effective—letter.

Type up your penciled copy so that you can see a whole page at a time. Triple space this draft to allow for reactions, insertions, deletions. Give yourself room for changes. If you're not a typist, write on every second or third line. Leave plenty of white space for those very necessary revisions.

Write or type on one side of the paper only to allow for changes and rearrangements through cutting and pasting. This saves retyping or recopying time, lets you put your effort into what you have to say. Of course, a word processor does this work for you—on command.

Read your copy aloud. Or read it into a cassette recorder and then listen to it without looking at the printed page. Let your ear respond to the flow of ideas, the rhythm of the language, or, conversely, catch an awkward or confusing phrase or expression. "The ear does it," claimed Robert Frost, who surely knew. "The ear is the only true writer and the only true reader."

Test your copy on carefully selected others. Choose a friendly yet critical ear. You want good, helpful feedback, but your fragile writer's ego also needs moral support. Here is where a writing group really helps—an understanding and

BENJAMIN FRANKLIN TELLS HOW HE DEVELOPED AS A WRITER

About this time I met with an old Volume of the Spectator. It was the Third. I had never before seen any of them. I bought it, read it over and over, and was much delighted with it. I thought the Writing excellent, and wish'd if possible to imitate it. With that View, I took some of the Papers, and making short Hints of the Sentiment in each Sentence, laid them by a few Days, and then without looking at the Book, try'd to compleat the Papers again, by expressing each hinted Sentiment at length, and as fully as it had been express'd before, in any suitable Words, that should come to hand.

Then I compar'd my Spectator with the Original, discover'd some of my Faults and corrected them. But

knowledgeable audience is what you want.

Put your draft aside. Walk away from it to do something else—push-ups, dishes, sleep. Give yourself some time. Then return to it. You will find that even though your conscious mind turned it off, your subconscious didn't. You'll come back with a fresh eye and ear.

I found I wanted a Stock of Words or a Readiness in recollecting and using them, which I thought I should have acquir'd before that time, if I had gone on making Verses, since the continual Occasion for Words of the same Import but of different Length, to suit the Measure, or of different Sound for the Rhyme, would have laid me under a constant Necessity of searching for Variety, and also have tended to fix that Variety in my Mind, and make me Master of it. Therefore I took some of the Tales and turn'd them into Verse: And after a time, when I had pretty well forgotten the Prose, turn'd them back again. I also sometimes jumbled my Collections of Hints into Confusion, and after some Weeks, endeavour'd to reduce them into the best Order, before I began to form the full Sentences, and compleat the Paper. This was to teach me Method in the Arrangement of Thoughts. By comparing my work afterwards with the original, I discover'd many faults and amended them; but I sometimes had the Pleasure of Fancying that in certain Particulars of small Import, I had been lucky enough to improve the Method or the Language and this encourag'd me to think I might possibly in time come to be a tolerable English Writer, of which I was extreamly ambitious.

Writing Warmups

Even though you find an ideal place and want very much to get started, writing, like exercise, doesn't always go easily. Some days you'll be stiff, reluctant, tired, or lazy. Even the experts have trouble at times. While working on his novel *East of Eden*, John Steinbeck began each morning's session by writing a letter to his editor. The letters (later published as *A Journal of a Novel: The East of Eden Letters*) served as a warmup, a getting into gear. In one of them Steinbeck says, "I don't understand why some days are wide open and others closed off, some days smile and others have thin slitted eyes and others still are days which worry."

On almost any day, but especially on days that don't smile, you will find something on this list to help you warm up and get started:

Quick Starts—Serious and Zany

Write an essay about your toes.

Are you a pessimist or an optimist? Why?

The city has given you a billboard to fill with a different message on each of seven days. What will you write on it?

Write a letter to your dog.

Complain for five minutes.

What makes you laugh?

When you were a child, what things lurked under your bed or in your closet?

Write down as many cliche's as you can think of in ten minutes.

Do you like the way you look? How would you change yourself?

Why are you so blah today?

Imagine yourself as an animal—what would you be and why?

*You are allowed to write fifty words to be enclosed
   in a time capsule that will be opened in the year
   2076. What will you write?*
*Write down in ten minutes as many things as you
   can that you know for sure about yourself.*
*What are you doing sitting in that chair at this
   time?*
If you could be anywhere in the world now, where
   would you be? Why?
What did you dream about last night, or the night
   before?
It's always raining somewhere on earth.
Describe what you see beyond the houses of your
   eyes.

—Courtesy of Richard Behm

Warmups can produce some interesting consequences.
Ray brought the black iron gadget photographed below to his

writing class and asked the members to write about it. They passed the "curlecue" around, fingering and turning it, standing it up, trying to fit it into their grasp. Then they wrote—laughingly guessing that it was a gear, brass knuckles, an apple peeler, an artist's misconception. Ray persisted. His query to *Yankee Magazine*'s authority on antiques brought the answer . . .

Plain Talk
by Earl Proulx

12-18-84

Dear Mr. Hager;
What you have has known as a "Cook's answer".
sold to Farm wives and ships Cooks as an
answer to all their problems.
    The two rings are finger holes, and the long
hook was to lift stove lids. The four prongs
were for tenderizing meat. The smaller hooks were
for picking up pots and kettles by the bails
when they were hot. Laid flat on the table it
served as a trivet for a hot dish.
    If a Tramp came to the farm house door it
could be used as brass knuckles to scare
him away. or worn while serving coffee, it
kept the complaints down.
                        Happy Holidays
                        Earl Proulx

For Further Development

You've finished your warmup; you're ready for more strenuous exercise. And that's what the next set of suggestions will provide. They are designed for practice, of course, but with specific writing skills in mind.

Sounding off   Try a version of Steinbeck's warmup. Write a letter you don't intend to send. Tell a friend or foe what you think of modern movies (violent? explicit? innovative?). Or what you think of television ads (intrusive? clever? sexy?)

Selecting the right word   Consider each group of words below. They are often cited as synonyms. Yet, are they interchangeable? What differences come to mind? Under what circumstances would each word be appropriate? Add other words to each list if you wish.

1. progeny
   kid
   brat
   offspring
   bambino
   heir
   child

2. devilish
   incorrigible
   naughty
   mean
   bad
   wicked
   improper

3. meal
   spread
   mess
   feast
   smorgasbord
   barbecue
   banquet

4. respect
   adoration
   consideration
   homage
   worship
   reverence
   esteem

Observing closely

Watching your cat Samantha is one of your favorite indoor sports. Describe her movements and poses and purrs this morning.

Forming and giving opinions

You read the morning paper with your first cup of coffee. You're still bristling over the exposé of sports star excesses. Or that article about government leaders who refer to nuclear weapons as "peacekeepers." React in writing.

Look at this May 24, 1847, list from the journals of Ralph Waldo Emerson. He is musing about people's concerns and attitudes:

Philosophizing

The Superstitions of our Age:
  The fear of pauperism;
  The fear of immigration;
  The fear of manufacturing interests;
  The fear of radicalism or democracy;
  And faith in the steam engine.

What do you consider the superstitions of our age? What would you include? Some of the same items? And are they all superstitions? Using Emerson's entry as a model, compile your own list.

Consider this "momentous" happening reported by the Manchester, Iowa, press sometime in the seventies:

Suiting style
to point
of view

> ## 2 Seek Damages Totaling $12,670 in Bull Incident
>
> Leon Offerman and William Bonert have filed separate damage suits totaling $12,670.75 in Delaware county district court in connection with an alleged loose bull incident.
>
> Defendant in each suit is Henry Bockenstedt.
>
> Offermann is seeking judgment of $7,698.25 in one petition and Bonert is asking for damages of $4,974.50 in another suit.
>
> The suits stem from an incident which occurred on Sept. 8, 1974 when a bull owned by the defendant allegedly broke through or jumped a fence into a pasture rented by the plaintiffs.
>
> The bull allegedly bred 25 purebred Holstein heifers owned by the plaintiffs.
>
> Offermann and Bonert are claiming negligence against the defendant and are asking for the separate damages listed above.

The writing here is fairly straight reporting. So let's try some other approaches and look at this event from different points of view. Retell the story from the standpoint of the presiding judge, the angry defendants, the much-maligned owner, the smiling young bull, one of the "fallen" heifers, a bemused "what fools these mortals be" courtroom spectator. Select one of these— or any other. See what happens to the "facts in the case."

Many of the activities we have suggested to help you develop as a writer invite you to observe carefully and then to put your observations into the best possible words. Joseph Conrad, a Polish author who wrote in English, put it this way: "My task which I am trying to achieve is, by the power of the written word, to make you hear, to make you feel—it is before all, to make you see. That—and no more, and it is everything." A tall order. But that is what good writing is.

Part II

Writing— More or Less Personal

Chapter 3

Lists—Leading Somewhere

*Y*ou have made hundreds of lists—some important, some mere doodling. Most of them went somewhere or helped you get somewhere. You took them along to the grocery store, used them for check-off in planning a day, preparing for a trip, setting agenda for a meeting, or addressing your Christmas cards; or maybe you just referred to them to jog a less than perfect memory. No matter how little you write, you probably find lists very important day-to-day writing.

But lists are more than just practical items for checking. They prevent forgetting and save time and mistakes, of course, but they also are often the basis for meaningful discourse. A list may start as practicality, mere amusement, something to do in an idle moment. And then you may discover in it some shape, some meaning. For instance, the popular song from *The Sound of Music* is a list concluding with the words "These are a few of my favorite things." Humorist Andy Rooney got an entire column out of a list he entitled "It's Just One Darn Thing After Another":

The following things are hard to do

Get in your car when someone has parked too close to you on the driver's side.

Tear something along the dotted line when the instructions read "Tear Along Dotted Line."

Carry a couch upstairs if you're the one walking backwards.

Draw a circle freehand.

Let down a Venetian blind the first time without pulling the cord this way and that.

Tie a necktie so it comes out even at the ends.

Put the ice cube trays back in the freezer without spilling water.

Replace the screens with the storm windows—or the storm windows with the screens.

Get the color right again on the television once you've messed it up.

Cut the fingernails of your right hand with your left hand if you're right-handed or vice versa.

Reach for the towel when you get out of the shower without getting water all over the bathroom floor.

Turn over the mattress.

Get the car in the garage without hitting some of the junk you've got stored along the side.

Take something out of your eye without your glasses on—which you've had to take off to get at what's in your eye.

Get off a crowded elevator at the second floor of an eight-floor store when you were the first one on.

Wash a pan you've scrambled eggs in.

Keep from getting distracted by another newspaper story when you're looking for the continuation on page nine of a story you started on page one.

Open the back door when you're carrying two bags of groceries.

Get up and go to bed if you fall asleep on the couch watching television.

Swallow a pill by taking a drink from a fountain you have to bend over to get at.

Remember when you last put a battery in your watch.

Get anything out of your pants pocket when you have your seatbelt fastened.

Find the light switch in a dark room.

Keep your hands from smelling like gas when you help yourself at a self-service gas station.

Take all the pins out of a new shirt.

Pack a suitcase for warm weather when you're starting from a cold place.

Get all the peanut butter out of the jar.

Get rid of the toothpick after you've eaten an hors d'oeuvre at a cocktail party.

Quit a job you hate if the money's good.

Know what to do with all the wires from two lamps, a record player and the television set.

Lists Leading to Meaning

Eggs
sugar
tomatoes; lettuce
frozen lemonade
mustard
Tide
coffee!
apricots

Even a grocery list might add up to mean something. This one suggests that you are about to run out of staples. Can you devise a list to suggest writing an essay with one of these opening sentences?

- My grocery list reflects changes of seasons.
- Some prices at the supermarket are actually going down (or surely going up).
- Shopping for a healthful diet is becoming easier.
- Shopping for one is a challenge.

The phrase "It's all in a day" might open a journal entry after you'd made a list such as this one. Or "I certainly can blow a lot of money fast." Try a similar list and writing task for yourself; have a bit of fun with it.

Dentist — 10 a.m.
Call re. Car insurance
Send IRS check
Order cedar chips
for flower beds
Pick up cleaning

Listing Gives Perspective

This list from Morton P. Kelsey, author of *The Other Side of Silence: A Guide to Christian Meditation*, shows how listing helps keep values in order. If you made a similar list, what would you include?

> One of the best ways I have found of keeping myself reminded of the importance of these times alone is to keep a list of things that are important to me in order to see just how I do use my time. Generally, I put them down like this:
>
> My family—my wife, children, and their families.
> Those toward whom I have special responsibility.
> My friends.
> My students and counselees—time spent in meeting with students.
> My religious practice, my time for God, for the Eucharist.
> My teaching, the reading that keeps me current, and research.

My writing, organizing what I have learned to
share with a larger group.
My lecturing.
My recreation, time to rest and to play, to enjoy
life and be recreated.
My sleep.

Lists Become Poems

More will be said about lists when we get to the chapter on writing poems, but stop here for a minute to discover how some poems might begin in the association of items that come together in a list. John Ciardi in his book *How Does a Poem Mean?* says some poems are catalogues. He considers Walt Whitman's "I Hear America Singing" as such a list-poem, and says that Mrs. Browning's famous love sonnet simply lists the answers to the question in its first line title:

How do I love thee? Let me count the ways.
I love thee to the depth and breadth and height
My soul can reach, when feeling out of sight
For the ends of being and ideal grace.
I love thee to the level of every day's
Most quiet need, by sun and candle-light.
I love thee freely, as men strive for right.
I love thee purely, as they turn from praise.
I love thee with the passion put to use
In my old griefs, and with my childhood's faith.
I love thee with a love I seemed to lose
With my lost saints. I love thee with the breath,
Smiles, tears, of all my life; and, if God choose,
I shall but love thee better after death.

You may not want to write poetry, but if you do, look ahead to the chapter on poetry and see how lists might become triggers for your poems.

Lists Lead to Essays

A list can be the heart of an essay. In this column entitled "Swapping Detergents, and Other Mistakes You Won't Repeat," Sheila Taylor frames a list with an introduction and an ending comment to point up its purpose.

A reader keeps nagging me to write a column about mistakes you aren't likely to repeat. To get me started, she reminds me of the one she made that she'll never, never make again. She substituted washing machine detergent for dishwasher detergent.

"It was an emergency situation," she says. "I thought it wouldn't hurt. It did."

On the other hand, after all the suds subsided, she ended up with the cleanest kitchen floor in Texas. The cleanest dining room floor, too. Also, the cleanest living room and entry hall floors. "Ah. And my ceilings, they fairly sparkled," she adds.

Someone else says the mistake he won't make again was treating the red-light warning on his dashboard a shade too lightly.

"I was fairly new to driving and thought it was an early warning signal, rather than a LOOK OUT! signal. Disaster. Instant, expensive disaster," he recalls.

I once cooked a frozen Mexican dinner in the oven upside down, and spent the next 10 years cleaning the mess from the bottom of the oven. Even so, that experience pales when compared to another.

As a newlywed, I removed a large hen from the oven one morning, put it on the counter and took off on errands with the little mister while the chicken cooled. We ran into friends and ended up spending the entire day and most of the evening away from home.

When we returned to our small apartment, well, to this day, 25 years and four houses later, I cannot cut up a cooked chicken without that same odor seeping from the walls to envelop me in a cloud of nausea. We seldom have chicken salad at our house.

Other Mistakes One Isn't Likely to Repeat:

Transforming jeans or casual pants into cut-offs or shorts without measuring each leg first.

Giving yourself a haircut.

Coloring your hair yourself without first doing a "patch" test. Actually, that's a mistake most people don't repeat. Unfortunately, I have many times. But not lately.

Not looking to see if the container spout is secure before sprinkling salt into a batter or pot of something or other.

Assuming the flue is open before lighting the first fire of the season.

Assuming you know who's on the other end of the phone before you start wisecracking.

Assuming "dry clean only" is nothing more than a get-rich ploy for the cleaners' industry, although I have hand-washed many a silk blouse and nightie with no harm done.

Telling the boss you can be reached at home during your vacation. Next time, say you'll be in Munich.

Not tasting the salsa first.

Being, shall we say, careless on your tax return.

Calling someone a jerk without looking around first.

Not believing a "tow away zone" sign.

Not waiting for the baby to burp.

Letting your kid eat a chocolate ice-cream cone in the car.

Assuming your gas gauge errs on the side of caution.

Walking through plate glass doors without checking to see if they're open.

Alas, some mistakes we keep repeating, as though we were programmed to err in a particular manner. Every year, we stay too long on the beach, even though we know for dead certain we'll pay the price of agony, and we fall in love for the wrong reasons over and over again, and we're suckers for the same fantastic financial deal we fell for the last time.

Every week, I try to carry in all my groceries at once, and every week, I either mop up broken eggs, chase rolling oranges under the car or cry over spilt milk.

What's more, I'll probably do the same again this afternoon. I know I will, because I'll also know that this time I can manage just one more bag.

Notice how this *New Yorker* writer, featured in the "Talk of the Town" section, apparently shaped the idea for an essay from the annual list of hurricane names. Within the essay, too, the writer makes use of still another list.

Partly Cloudy

We have in our possession the list of hurricane names for the next few seasons. Next fall, Hurricane Fabian. The year after that, Ivan, Mitch, and Shary, forcing the cancellation of more events than you thought possible, flooding your basement, knocking your tree over on top of your garage. It's in 1987, though, that the sky really darkens. If we reach Hurricane Wilma, it will be only because we've weathered Bret, Floyd, Harvey, Lenny, Nate, Stan, and Vince, among others. Not Stanley— Stan. Do you want your valuable beachfront property washed away by a Hurricane Vince? Write the people at the National Oceanic and Atmospheric Administration, and write them today.

Two Urban Park Rangers, at sprawling Van Cortlandt Park, in the Bronx, told us about the hurricanes, and about other, subtler forms of weather. "Everyone is a weatherman," said Jeffrey Freilich, one of the rangers. "If you open your door, and you look outside, and you say, 'Hey, it's going to rain,' then you're a meteorologist. If you spit on your finger and hold it up in the wind, you're a meteorologist." He told us to picture the planet as a sphere, and people as crabs crawling about its surface beneath an ocean of air. That ocean is where the weather is. Then he and his colleague, Robert Burgio, told us how to predict the weather— information worth passing along. It will be winter if:

Muskrat houses are built big.
Cow's hooves break off early.
Screech owls sound like women crying.
Crows "gather together."
Worms begin crawling into abandoned houses in October.
Wild hogs gather sticks, straws, or shucks to make a bed.
Carrots grow deeper than usual.
Sweet potatoes have a tougher skin.
The fur on the bottom of a rabbit's foot is thicker.

We believe everything the Rangers told us, but

urban living has so atrophied our instincts that the hints may never help us. We did not know (we would like to say we have forgotten, but that would be a lie) that cows' hooves break off at all, much less at some predictable moment. In fact, we're so citified that the thought alarms us a little. As for screech owls crying like women, what if you hear a sound like a woman crying? Suppose you go investigate and find it's not a screech owl at all but a woman crying. What then?

Lists in Your Life— to Do and to Think about

1) Individually or in a small group, make a list of "useful lists" or "lists in my life." Hold a discussion or write a short paper about the uses you make of lists.

2) Write a paragraph or two in response to one of these suggestions:
> I don't know what I'd do if I lost (you name the) list.
> How do lists control us?
> Are card files or notebooks best for (some kind of list—you choose)?
> The most important list I ever made was _____ .
> Making a list might help (me, someone, in some way).

3) We have many associations with Christmas lists or birthday books or records, with lists of club members, church organization rolls, etc. Talk (or think) about the meaning of these lists, or of one particular list, in your life. Write a short paper about the surprises or memories in such a list, or about how it may be changing over the years.

4) Look along your bookshelf or at the library for books that are essentially lists. Begin with some of the "how to" or "reasons for" publications. Consider how the authors have used the lists to structure their books. Are some arranged in

order of importance—first, second, or third? Are some simple chronology? Discuss or think about the list as a way of organizing writing.

5) Look out a window or around a room and jot down the items you observe. Then use the list as a step to a paragraph summing up the impression of the scene. This exercise helps you both remember and organize details.

6) Mary Ellen Chase, known for novels and for her widely read *The Bible for the Common Reader,* kept a "word list," noting words that she liked, wanted to go back to and think about. Such a list is a wonderful vocabulary builder, but it is also an interesting game for word-lovers. Try one yourself, jotting down intriguing words you hear and read.

7) Make a book list for some special reader—a handicapped friend, a grandchild, a group of friends who gather to talk about reading, your senior citizens' club, a Sunday School class.

8) Here is a potpourri of subjects for free-association lists (random thoughts plus random notes):
- things I treasure (antiques, memories, photographs, etc.)
- things I'd like to throw out
- things I wish I'd kept
- my favorite places (parks, restaurants, scenes, etc.), or places where I wish I'd lived
- questions I'd like to ask _____
  (fill the blank with the name of a person or group)
- questions no one has ever answered for me

9) Read again the list Morton P. Kelsey made of things he values. What do you learn about the writer from his list? How might a list of things you value reveal you as a person? Would your list be different at different times of your life? Make such a list or lists, and consider how they might serve as the basis for

autobiography or biography. File this exercise away to use again when you decide to write a memoir or a character sketch of someone you know.

10) Some final fun—and proof that lists really go somewhere. Go back after reading the chapter and devise a list of your own to use as point of departure for a short essay. You might try a title like "It's Just One Bit of Good Luck After Another," or "It's Just One Complaint After Another." Or you might use the list of places where you wish you had lived or one of places you have visited and write on "Dream Towns."

These suggestions are, of course, just that—suggestions. Take off—*list* off in any direction you like. Remember—lists go somewhere! In fact, almost anywhere.

Chapter 4

Journals, Logs, Diaries

*P*erhaps you once kept a log of a week's camping trip as a step toward a Boy Scout merit badge. Or your brother gave you a five-year diary for Christmas and then he stole it after you'd crammed its pages with secrets. A business appointment book or a club calendar, a farm or garden planting record, a health record of "Baby's First Seven Years," the notes on the progress of a scientific experiment—all sorts of things are journals of some kind, kept for various purposes at various times.

As you get older, you may have less record-keeping, but a journal—kept steadily or intermittently—can be surprisingly beneficial. Whether you jot a few lines in a "Daily Planner," or write extensively in a brightly bound booklet, or accumulate typed sheets to add to a loose-leaf file, consider these benefits. A journal can be many things:

1) *a record*—almost any type.

As such, it serves to keep things straight, acts as a memory jogger. But it does much more: it becomes an archive, a treasured source of history, providing facts and chronology for later use. Travel writer Freya Stark thought a journal was a way to take a journey over again, to make it *perennial*.

2) *a friend*—one always at hand, one to trust.

With the act of writing you talk to your friend on paper. The journal listens whether you are happy or sad, troubled or angry, clever and funny, or repetitive and boring.

3) *a therapist*—like a doctor or nurse, an aid to health.

As outlet or release, a journal often helps clarify emotions, recognize strengths and weaknesses, give new and needed perspectives. Or a journal may become a health record for guiding exercise or diet.

4) *a teacher*—a guide to learning and growing.

Just as school notebooks are a way of organizing, of sifting the important, and of learning, so a journal becomes a way of noting and reacting to events, other people's comments, thousands of subjects. A journal may be a log or diary summarizing your reading and gathering memorable quotes or ideas; it may be devoted to analysis of a policy or decision; it could take the form of notes about a project or a hobby that you are trying to master.

5) *a draft*—a place to practice writing.

This is, of course, a book about writing, and your journal may provide a first step toward writing that you wish to do. Innumerable writers—in fact, almost all writers—keep a journal of some sort. Many famous published journals are those of writers, and from reading their notebooks we discover much about their sources, where they found ideas, and how they went about the work of writing.

—Nathaniel Hawthorne's journal observations of his daughter Una provided the details that he used in describing the child Pearl in *The Scarlet Letter.*

—Henry David Thoreau, who kept a journal almost all his life, first described details of daily living at Walden Pond in his records for the months he lived there. Revised, embellished, distilled, that journal became the basis for his great work, *Walden.*

—In her journal Virginia Woolf described the experience behind the lectures that eventually became *A Room of One's Own.*

Hawthornes, Woolfs, and Thoreaus are few and far between, but even if you aren't in that league, it is worth keeping a journal as a way to develop your ability as a writer. Here you write without criticism. Here you can collect, try out various ways of expressing, scratch out and add without organizing or feeling constraints. What is more, writing becomes easier—and more fun—as you do it.

Diaries—
Many Varieties, Many Sizes

Joseph Reynolds, a free-lance writer and teacher, claims,

> *My journal is a storehouse, a treasury for everything in my daily life: the stories I hear, the people I meet, the quotations I like, and even the subtle signs and symbols I encounter that speak to me indirectly. Unless I capture these things in writing, I lose them.*

Carol Krucoff says,

> *Before there were analysts' couches, encounter groups, rolfing and primal-scream therapies,*

*people who wanted to put their lives in perspective
often wrote their thoughts and feelings and dreams
in a journal.*

Henry David Thoreau wrote,

> *"Says I to myself" should be the motto of my
> journal.*

Dorothy Lambert says,

> *A journal may be all gems, or all logs, or all plans
> and blueprints, or all test tubes, or all confession, or
> all collections of oddments—or it may be a marvel-
> ous hodgepodge of the old-fashioned general store.*

Morton P. Kelsey, author of *The Other Side of Silence: A
Guide to Christian Meditation*, writes,

> *It is difficult for many people to quiet their minds.
> As soon as they begin to center down, ideas start to
> come up that jar them out of the silence. . . . My
> own experience is that it is difficult to come to
> silence until I have paid these aspects of myself their
> due. With a journal and a pencil ready, I start by
> looking at the circumstances that have been both-
> ering me. As I write down whatever comes to mind
> about them, often bubbling up helter-skelter, they
> begin to lose their power over me. The concerns are
> no less important. They will be there when I get
> back to regular activity, but I know by experience
> that I will have a fresh outlook about them because
> of touching a level beyond my ordinary ego life.
> Keeping a record that gives a before and after look
> is a tremendous help to me in slowing down and
> ceasing activity. In one way it is a symbol reminding
> me that I have an appointment with stillness.*

DEAR DIARY—

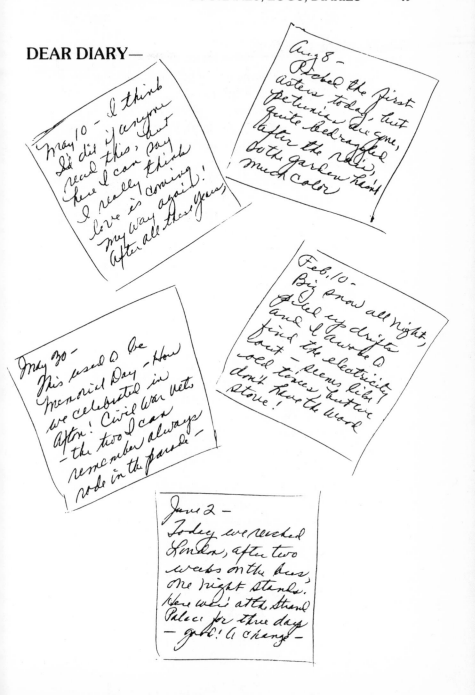

Journals for Reading

Journals make intriguing reading. You might like Hal Borland's *Book of Days* and Edith Holden's *A Country Diary of An Edwardian Lady,* which were written seventy years apart but both published in 1976. Borland, long a nature writer for *The New York Times,* observed the "natural year" on his Connecticut farm. He calls his journal his "day-to-day thinking about this world around me and my fellow creatures here." Edith Holden, the Edwardian lady, wrote about life in the English countryside in 1906. She decorated her pages with small paintings of the birds, butterflies, bees and flowers she described, and she introduced bits of philosophy by jotting quotations and poems she liked. Her book became a treasure house for herself, one shared with the world only after many years.

From Hal Borland's *Book of Days*

May 12
The whippoorwills have returned to the valley. I heard one calling last evening. It seemed late until I looked in my records and found that the earliest I ever heard one here was April 24 and the latest was the last week in May. So May's second week seems to be about average.

We have had whippoorwills every year that we have been here, though there have been fewer as the years pass. Just over the mountain from us, however, they seem to have no whippoorwills at all. I don't know why. We certainly have no monopoly on the night insects on which whippoorwills feed. I suspect that they come down here at night because the lights in the house attract insects, particularly moths. But there are houses over there, too.

Usually I am glad to have the whippoorwills around. Now and then they come down too close to the house and sound off too long and too loudly, particularly at 3:00 a.m. One of them, a few years ago, chose to perch on the woodshed just back of the house and call for half an hour at a time at that infernal hour. But the past few years they have all kept to the woodland and even when I waken and hear them I can go back to sleep. Sometimes I count whippoorwill calls instead of sheep. My record is 546 calls by the same bird without more than momentary pauses for breath. John Burroughs once counted more than 1,300 calls in such a sequence.

May 14

This is a day when I choose to quote from something I wrote some years ago. It goes thus:

We all have our summation days, when we draw a figurative line and tot up both the year and the years. I am not summarizing today, however. I am thinking how fortunate I am, how much any child of mid-May has to be thankful for. When he is young he can say: "The robin sings for me, and the oriole, and the lilacs bloom today. The trout are eager in the brook. Summer is not yet here, but close at hand. My years begin with song."

When he comes to middle age he can say, "Another winter is over and gone, and the earth resumes its vigor. My years are like the season, at their flowering, new growth on old stems and the strength of maturity in the trunk."

And when the years amount to age he can say, "I have seen the season turn with the sun, all my days, and each year I feel the growing warmth as my world turns green. My years are spring, all of them, spring returning like a promise and a fragrant fulfillment."

From Edith Holden's *A Country Diary of An Edwardian Lady*

MAY

'Then came faire May, the fairest mayde on ground;
Deckt all with dainties of her seasons pryde,
And throwing flowers out of her lap arounde;
Upon two Brethren's shoulders she did ride;
The Twins of Leda, which on eyther side,
Supported her like to their soveraine queene:
Lord! How all creatures laught when her they spide;
And leapt and daunc't as they had ravish't beene!
And Cupid selfe about her fluttered all in greene.'

Spenser

May 11. Saw a dead Hedge-hog curled up by the roadside.

12 Went to Stratford on Avon, and walked to Shottery across the meadows. On the way I gathered Hawthorn blossom from the hedges, and saw fields yellow with Buttercups and banks of blue Speedwell. The Dandelions were a wonderful sight along the railway cutting.

14 Visited the violet-wood this evening; it is quite green and shady there now, as most of the trees are Firs and Sycamores and the latter are in full leaf. The ground was covered with Wild Arums, all in flower, — their pale green spathes gleaming out very conspicuously against the red earthen banks where the rabbits burrow. Some of the sheathes were spotted and I found one deep, reddish purple in colour. The large, handsome green leaves that were so beautiful in the early spring, are now beginning to wither away, as the flowers attain maturity.
I noticed the flower just coming on the Beech, scarcely distingu-ishable from the tender green of the foliage. Oak-apples are plentiful now on the Oak-trees.

The journals of many famous persons and some not so famous often have literary or historical value in themselves, or they are primary source materials for biographers and historians, but most of us never keep a journal that sees print. That doesn't mean, though, that the journal habit isn't worthwhile. Edgar Harrison, the editor of *Good Old Days*, known as "the magazine that remembers the best," confirms that value in this editorial that he wrote about rediscovering a diary he had kept as a boy.

Every once in a while, my wife Mollie feels the urge to have a rummage sale. It seems kind of fruitless to me; she sells our old junk to other people and then in turn buys their old junk when they have a sale. We don't end up with any less junk; we just trade.

When she gets the rummage sale urge, she makes me go through my garage, my drawers, my study, and my corners of the basement and attic. For years I used to pretend I really was sorting through my treasures by puttering around and moving a few things. Sometimes, I'd just nap for a half hour or so and then tell her I hadn't found anything I wanted to part with. She eventually caught me and now she "helps" me sort.

Recently, she was going through a box which contained items from my school days. "Do you want this?" she'd ask. "Yes," I'd say. "Whatever for? It's so ratty (dirty, old, grubby, tacky, etc.)!" "Because I want it, that's why!" and so forth.

Eventually, she pulled out an old book that was all of ratty, dirty, old, grubby and tacky and announced, "You surely don't want this, too!" When I saw that little brown book with its cover half torn off, my heart gave a leap. Excitedly, I grabbed it. It was my old journal from my childhood-teenage days.

I opened the first page. It read: Unfair, unfair, unfair! Mama is just plain unfair! *Ah, yes, I remembered. I'd ruined my Sunday shirt and Mother had spanked me. I thought I was too big to be spanked but Mother thought otherwise. I flipped through the pages. Dad had taken me hunting and I shot my first squirrel. I must have been delirious with joy as I reported that it* made good eating *and I don't even like squirrel. As I paged toward the back, I noticed how my handwriting improved and matured. I saw cryptic references to my secret heartthrob Lucille and an announcement of my first shave. In places, there were large gaps of time between entries. Other times, I chronicled for weeks. Abruptly, the notations came to an end. I wondered why, when there were clean pages left, I had quit writing in the book. Somewhere, I had outgrown this journal and had gone on to a new one.*

As I closed my old journal, I saw Mollie putting the last items back into the box. "There's some room on top for that," she told me. I slipped it in and she shut the box.

"Did you find anything there for your sale?" I asked her.

"No, it's all valuable things," she said smiling at me.

She's right, of course. Anything that brings back the memories of the Good Old Days is too valuable to be sold.

A Few Tips for Journal Keepers

- Get a notebook of the kind and size that invites you to write.

- Set aside a time for writing, but don't feel enslaved by it even though accumulation is the point of keeping a journal. Make that time enjoyable; avoid times when you are too tired to care.

- Write enough to satisfy your purpose. You may start too big, too enthusiastically, then find a satisfactory length a little later. Length of entries will vary from day to day.

- Put in what really interests you. After a few days look back and ask yourself, "Will I enjoy rereading this sometime next year?" Even just to yourself, it is pleasant to come off as a vital, thinking person.

- Include details. They make your pictures memorable and help you recall when you reread. Think of your journal as a place to tell a reader interesting tidbits about your days.

- Write freely; play with words. Don't worry about mechanics—spelling, punctuation, sentences—at this point.

And Try These for Getting Started

1) If you hesitate and wonder, "Will I really benefit from keeping a journal?" you might like to read about Ira Progoff, who conducts journal workshops and has published books about what keeping a journal can do for people. He says that the privacy of journals will allow people to "push into themselves" and discover how much they know, look at things more objectively, and clarify their emotions and values. Write out your feelings and thoughts for a few days. Look the material over. Determine how and why the writing may help you. Share your experience if you wish, or keep it strictly private.

2) If you are bubbling with plans for future action—ideas for places to go or things to do, hobbies to pursue, or just anything—try writing about them. Each day for a week, write about one of these plans or wishes. Then sift through and decide which to carry out. Both the writing and the planning can be exhilarating.

3) If you have enjoyed some activity with a friend—taken a trip, attended a play or concert, gone to a banquet or picnic, gone to an antique mall or a flower show, etc.—challenge that friend to "write it up" and do the same yourself. Exchange your journal entries and talk about how each of you captured the experience. You'll probably find that you noticed different things and had different reactions.

4) Keep a record for a few days for someone away—a friend in another state, a relative who is in the hospital, someone who hasn't shared an interesting experience or event. Your journal entry may become the basis for a fascinating letter, or perhaps a renewal of an association.

5) After listening to the commentary on television or radio on the day's news, try writing your own comments on personal, local, or national events of the day. Do this for a week; almost certainly your comments will become sharper, more discerning, and perhaps funnier.

6) Use your journal as a garden record, a weather record, an outdoor activity record, or write some other observations of nature over the next couple of weeks. Ask yourself, "Am I noticing more?" You probably will be!

Chapter 5

The Art and Joy of Writing Letters

*S*omewhere we read a story about a little boy who returned an overdue notice with his library book. "May I keep the letter?" he asked the librarian. "It's the first one I ever had." Many of you have had such a response to a letter—you just want to keep it. Emily Dickinson wrote this poem about her feeling of being transported to heaven by a letter from someone whose identity she doesn't reveal.

> *The way I read a letter's this*
> *'Tis first I lock the door,*
> *And push it with my fingers next,*
> *For transport it be sure.*
>
> *And then I go the furthest off*
> *To counteract a knock;*
> *Then draw my little letter forth*
> *And softly pick its lock.*

Then, glancing narrow at the wall,
And narrow at the floor,
For firm conviction of a mouse
Not exorcised before,

Peruse how infinite I am
To—no one that you know!
And sigh for lack of heaven,—but not
The heaven the creeds bestow.

Have you a box of letters you have never tossed out? A few love letters from an old suitor you can remember only vaguely? Some scrappy notes from your firstborn, eight years old and away at church camp? A letter your grandmother, living on a Kansas homestead, wrote to her mother "back East" after the birth of your father? If you have, you know that those treasures far outlast any long distance call, even though we all like to hear the warm voice that reaches out to touch across the miles.

Letters also reach out to touch across time. Phyllis and Obed Norem both saved the almost daily letters they wrote each other during World War II, when Obed was on duty in the Pacific and Phyllis was with her parents and small son in a midwestern town. Recently, Phyllis, now a widow and retired teacher, put the letters together with a little running commentary as a gift for the Norems' now grown-up children. The letters have become a family heirloom, a bit of real-life history.

Letters not only serve you personally, but they transact business. Even as we of the last part of the twentieth century begin to transmit business letters by computer, the need for composing remains. Orders, complaints, recommendations, queries—countless letters serve countless purposes. Advertisers, promoters, money raisers all know the value of tactfully and cleverly phrasing the letter to sell you something or win your support. Take a look at the junk mail you sometimes object to getting. Even all that has a purpose for someone who reaches out to touch.

Making It a Joy
to Open the Envelope

These tips should help you make your reader glad:

- Be spontaneous, direct, *yourself.*
  Write what you like—how you like it. If you let yourself have fun writing, the reader will enjoy what you write.

- Use interesting details; they *enliven.*

- Use informal (usually) and vivid words.
  Try for fresh expression, a new twist or a bit of humor.

- Suit tone to reader and purpose.
  Usually you can think of sharing, of enjoying together what you write; attitude shows in your tone. If you write for a serious purpose (to someone who has a problem, to settle a misunderstanding, etc.), then that consideration should control your tone.

- Plan, but not too much.
  Don't put in everything, and don't repeat or ramble. But don't be afraid to let ideas flow either.
- Try for a striking beginning, a friendly (humorous, if it is appropriate) closing. If you can, leave your reader with something to remember, something to keep.

Getting a letter means answering, for if you want to receive, it is blessed to give. Most of us can't clear the desk immediately after we get the mail, but if you want to correspond with someone it is often good to set a schedule. "You write the first week of the month and I'll write the third." We know of a Round Robin letter that has circulated among eleven friends for almost fifty years. The little bird is still flying because the writers, now living in eight different states and one foreign country, send on the letter two weeks after they receive it.

Letters to Enjoy—
and To Lead to Practice

Many people write "special occasion" letters, especially at Christmas or anniversaries or birthdays. Marge Warner gave hers a different flair, going back into family history rather than merely recounting the activities of the current year.

1981 CHRISTMAS GREETINGS   2933 ALGOMA ST.   STEVENS POINT WI 54481

It was in 1871, late in the summer, that thirteen-year old Hod left Island Pond, Vermont. He was headed for Wisconsin with his father (George W. Warner) and Frank Billiter. A covered wagon provided home and transportation on the long journey. Crammed in among their possessions were George's violin and Frank's large, gold harp.

The two men played for dances at frequent stops along the way. Hod's role was to collect a little loose change from all who danced. But he would accept a pocket knife in trade for admission from anyone who lacked money.

It was a slow trip in the cramped and creaking wagon. Early on Hod celebrated his fourteenth birthday. But the highlight of the trip came as the trio neared Chicago.

Smoke billowed above the city and the night sky glowed with a frightening red. It was October 8, 1871. Chicago was burning! Heat rose from the ashes and remnants of buildings smoldered as the travelers made their way north to a new home in Wisconsin.

Probably they reached it by November. That was when Hod unpacked the 137 knives he had put away - knives he had collected by sneaking people into the dances. And that was when word was sent to Hod's mother in Vermont that her husband and youngest child were safe and sound in Wisconsin at Plover in Portage County.

****

The picture was copied from a small and battered tintype. All I know about it is that at the left is Hod (Horace Nickerson) Warner and at the right is Frank Billiter (an Italian immigrant brought up by George W. and Elmina Warner).

I would suggest that it might have been taken shortly after their arrival in Plover and that it was sent to Hod's mother as proof of his safety. Wouldn't you agree that he appears to be a teenager and far short of his height as an adult?

It occurred to me that Hod Warner's descendants should hear about his covered wagon trip to Wisconsin and have a picture of him. So my Christmas greeting to you goes back 110 years to December when Hod was a new arrival in Plover and a pupil at the same school as eleven-year old Ida Richmond. They were married in Plover on September 30, 1880.

As you can see, Marge's letter invited responses. The relatives to whom she sent it might add stories of their own, or she might follow it up next year with additional details. Try some special "special occasions" of your own—

> A congratulatory letter to a bride and groom
> in which you describe a remembered wedding
> A birthday note with "famous happenings" from
> the same date
> A Christmas letter describing the time when
> something like the Grinch changed the holiday

You can think of others. But if you can't dream up a difference, write anyhow! Just be yourself and consider your reader.

It is good practice to think of different readers, for often we tell different things—give different impressions—to different people. Writing anything (just consider that advertising mail again—those writers know well the kind of appeal to "get" the reader) involves a triangle—

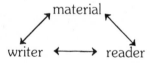

You, as writer, choose different details and use a different tone to reach your different readers. Writing for different audiences is good practice because it necessitates that you think about what you say and who will read what you say. This holds true for other forms of writing as well as for the letter, but letters are a good way to practice. Try one of these suggestions, and then see what Ella Morse did for her three readers.

1) You have a new car that you consider a lemon. Write a letter about it to

   • a person who has mentioned that he might buy a car of the same make
   • the auto company
   • a lawyer who is handling a claim beyond the warranty
   • the salesman who sold you the car

2) You were in an accident. You were the driver but no one was hurt badly. Write a letter explaining/describing the accident to

   • your insurance agent
   • a close friend
   • your son or daughter
   • the driver of the other car

3) You are a student in a program entitled "Silver Threads and Golden Pens." Write a letter describing the class to

   • your son or daughter, or a grandchild
   • a friend in another state
   • the director of a senior center that you think might initiate such a course

4) You have just retired and have been honored with several parties or a gift. Write about your feelings on these occasions to

   • a relative who lives in another state
   • one of the planners of the party or parties
   • a friend who is about to retire

5) While researching your family tree, you uncover a story about a distant cousin who was in prison for a robbery. Write a letter about it to

   • a grandchild
   • a friend who also is researching his/her family tree

• a cousin who has the delusion that the family is
  superior in every way

You could, of course, add to the list of topics for letters, or add
to the receivers for whom you write. Ella's letters here grew
out of the third suggestion.

Dear Director:

*Silver Threads and Golden Pens was truly an
inspiration. It gave us a real chance to say on paper
many things we dreamed of for years.*

*Perhaps it will help you to understand the value
of the class if you consider that in whichever
manner we have been employed there were always
considerations and obligations to duty which
created a restraint against free expression. Here
we are free to go where our pens and papers take
us. You might say we are creating a paper magic
carpet.*

*Some of us enjoy personal history which, of
course, is only a micro-image of a macro-world.
Some of us like experimental writing with experienced advice. At any rate while our numbers are
few, those of us who come to the meetings realize a
sense of fulfillment to ourselves that one could liken
to doing a good deed for the community. Thank you
for being our sponsor.*

Ella Morse

Dearest Sonny and Honey:

*Grams has enrolled in a personal writing class.
There are so many things which I felt you should
know about your forebears someday when you are
older and begin to wonder who and what we were. I*

hope to give you a realistic picture, for I do not believe it is wise to glamorize the past. The good old days are days that never were, and most of our past was made up of a combination of blood, sweat, tears, and brains, all applied to forge a better life for the future.

Love you both forever,
Grams

Dearest Old Friend:
I have decided to indulge in one of my oldest whims. I'm writing at a class which is led by professionals from the nearby University. We are really lucky to have such talent here at home. I guess something had to go "write" some day before we meet eternity.

You know, when one considers all the experiences we have had in our day, it would be superb to have you come visit here so we could share our notes and write cooperatively. I really hope to see you here in summer (if we have that day this cold year!).

Best always,
Ella

Enjoying Letters from the Archives

The archives of historical societies and libraries are full of what someone has called "epistolary treasures." Reading collected letters allows us glimpses of other lives, of other times and places. Here are two letters that bear the stamp of the individual writers and show awareness of the readers.

President Lincoln's letter to Mrs. Lydia Bixby—

> Executive Mansion
> Washington, Nov 21, 1864
>
> To Mrs Bixby, Boston, Mass,
>   Dear Madam.
>
>   I have been shown in the files of the War Department a statement of the Adjutant General of Massachusetts that you are the mother of five sons who have died gloriously on the field of battle I feel how weak and fruitless must be any word of mine which should attempt to beguile you from the grief of a loss so overwhelming. But I cannot refrain from tendering you the consolation that may be found in the thanks of the republic they died to save I pray that our Heavenly Father may assuage the anguish of your bereavement, and leave you only the cherished memory of the loved and lost, and the solemn pride that must be yours to have laid so costly a sacrifice upon the altar of freedom
>
>   Yours very sincerely and respectfully,
>   A. Lincoln.

Louisa May Alcott to her Mother—With a copy of her first book, *Flowers and Fables*

> *20 Pinckney Street, Boston, Dec. 25, 1854*
> *Dear Mother,—Into your Christmas stocking I have put my "first-born," knowing that you will accept it with all its faults (for grandmothers are always kind), and look upon it merely as an earnest of what I may yet do; for, with so much to cheer me on, I hope to pass in time from fairies and fables to men and realities.*
>
> *Whatever beauty or poetry is to be found in my little book is owing to your interest in and encouragement of all my efforts from the first to the last; and if ever I do anything to be proud of, my greatest happiness will be that I can thank you for that, as I may do for all the good there is in me; and I shall be content to write if it gives you pleasure.*
> *Jo is fussing about;*
> *My lamp is going out.*
> *To dear mother, with many kind wishes for a happy New Year and merry Christmas.*
> *I am your loving daughter*
> *Louy.*

Business Letters to Accomplish Your Purpose

Business letters are different. They usually go to an unknown audience—person or company—for a specific purpose. You write in order to achieve your business objective, although you want always to sound sincere—to be yourself. You will be more formal here, following accepted form and conventions. You may even use a manual to guide you in special cases.

Conventions are, of course, just current practices, not rigid rules. They change from time to time, for different kinds of letters, but these tips are useful for almost all business writing that you will do:

—Have a definite purpose, keep it firmly in mind as you write, and make it clear early in the letter. Reject anything not suited to that purpose. All this is a courtesy to your reader.

—Plan the points you want to make and give them a clear, easy-to-follow order.

—Write a draft whenever your letter needs special care or is to be very long; take care with the form, grammatical structures, and tone as you revise the draft for final copy.

—Keep a copy, either a carbon or a copy duplicated another way.

—Follow the conventional forms for the type of letter you are writing. These may include

- the place and date from which you write.
- an inside address—name, title, address of person to whom you write.
- a greeting or salutation, if you know the name of the addressee. (This often includes a title—Mr., Ms., Dean, Dr., etc.)
- complimentary close such as "Sincerely" or a similar phrase, with signature (full name) above your typed name. (Note: if you know the person addressed, you may address him as "Dear Joe," and sign with only your first name above your full typed name at close.)

Little differences, personal touches, help in business letters as they do in personal ones. You'll have fun reading this pair of letters, sent in sequence to a subscriber of *National Lampoon*. And you will notice again that letters reveal both the writer and the intended reader.

635 Madison Avenue, New York, N Y 10022
(212) 688-4070

We know what you did.

You know what you did.

And if you don't believe us, we have pictures of what you did.

So if you don't want everyone who reads the Lampoon to see what you did, you might seriously consider XXXXXXXXXXXXX resubscribing within the next twelve hours. We'd like to give you more time, but there are printing schedules that have to be observed. Hope you see things our way, but on the other hand, the pictures would make a pretty spicy cover.

Think it over.

                                        All the best,

                                        A Friend

Dear Subscriber:

A short while ago, we sent you a very funny reminder that your subscription to the *National Lampoon* was about to expire, and that if you wanted to continue to receive the magazine, you needed to make a renewal payment. You chose to ignore this amusing message.

Apparently, you have no sense of humor.

In view of that, let's approach the question of your subscription renewal from a different point of view.

In today's sophisticated world, a sense of humour is *de rigueur* for social or business success. "Gloomy Guses" and "Glenda Glums" just don't make the grade in the quick-witted America of the seventies. This is an era of fast comebacks, wisecracks, and flip replies. Wet blankets like you are passed over for important job promotions and sit home dateless while others, with their snappy patter, revel in new-found prosperity.

What can *you* do to preserve your job, your emotional attachments, and your prospects for the future? Well, fortunately for people like you, humor has its price. And the price is $7.95 for one year, $13.25 for two years, and $18.00 for three years. Careful study of each monthly edition of the *National Lampoon* will allow you to retain a semblance of drollery. But for $7.95 a year, don't expect miracles.

Yours truly,

Howard Jurofsky

Don't forget—when you say "Please write," you also say, "I'm pleased to write."

Part III

Writing—
Recollections
of the
Past

Chapter 6

Writing Short Memories

ike almost everyone else, you have probably said, "I'd like to put that in a novel," or "I've had some great experiences, some exciting ones." The kind of thing that seems as you look back to be terribly vivid, extremely funny, hauntingly sad, or just strikingly like the experiences of others may make a "little story," a bit of life worth retelling.

Writing "little memories" is like accumulating a scrapbook for yourself, but there are also many ways to share this kind of writing. Magazines and newspapers often feature "Yarns of Yesteryear," "what it was like back then." How often have you said in conversation, "Oh, that reminds me of the time the school bus broke down . . . "? Or, "That wedding we'll never forget—do you remember how Eileen was thirty minutes late and we all thought she'd changed her mind?" Or, "Just as the play was about to start, the ropes broke and the curtain couldn't be raised . . . "? Such remembered incidents are the basis for short published pieces.

What is more, psychologists seem to think such remembering is good for us as we grow older. In a *Psychology Today* article entitled "Mental Alertness and the Good Old Days," Joshua Fischman reports that gerontologists found real advantages for older persons who met in group reminiscing sessions once a week. Forty percent of those who participated showed improved short-term memory. Conjuring up memories and writing about them makes remembered people and events live again, and such writing can be a pleasure for you and a way of sharing the pleasure with others.

One Way to Start

By yourself or in a group, start small. Jot a few revealing details to picture your memory. In a group, talk about a single topic, passing it around so each person can recall particulars about that general subject. Then have a writing time so that you can put your recollections on paper. Or use the discussion as a trigger for writing later at home.

Here are three short pieces that came from a group where members discussed their memories of clothes.

1) Those red shoes in the window at Wahl's Store seemed to want to dance with me down the street, to wander in and out of my dreams, and to belong to me even before my mother could be convinced that I should go in to try them on. How I wanted those shoes! They would go with everything in my wardrobe. They would outshine all the other shoes in the Christmas program at Sunday School. I tried all the arguments, and I listened impatiently to the warnings that red shoes would not really be very practical. True, I needed new shoes for school, for running and kicking and climbing and everyday scuffling through mud puddles as all ten-year-olds do. But I begged—and finally my mother listened to me and we went to try the shoes.

They were perfect—just as I had known they would be—and with a little more talk and a bit of pinching and pushing of my toes by Gus, the shoe man, I went out with the new box proudly under my arm.

For several days I could do no more than admire the box and its contents on the closet shelf. Then came time for the first wearing—to the Christmas program. I marched back and forth, sang happily in the children's chorus of the Baby Jesus and the wisemen, sat and squirmed in a front pew where I was squeezed in a row of classmates, and often sneaked a glance at the shoes which marked a bright spot at the end of my long white cotton stockings.

On the way home, I dragged a little, walking a bit gingerly as Mother admonished that I hurry, it was cold. And a little later I remember that I felt relief and dismay as I pulled off the red shoes to find two bright pink blisters on my toes.

2) My mother's old photograph album captures the long-ago styles I still remember. Looking again at the black and white impressions of the small dark-eyed girl I once was, I can see clearly in color the dresses whose flounces and ruffles dominate those fading images. How well I remember the pink and white checked gingham with the wide white sash that was forever coming untied on my first day of school. I look determined but frightened in that pose on the porch steps just before I trudged off across the small park that separated our house from the old red brick school—a short distance to mark a big step in a child's world.

Another image recalls the soft smocked pongee, free-falling from narrow shoulders sunburned because we had been swimming at the lake, that I wore for my older half-sister's wedding. The flower-girl's basket with matching lining half tips, perhaps because of my excitement as I stood there worrying about doing everything just right, self-conscious because I was sure more people watched me than admired the bride.

And finally here is one of the fanciest and prettiest dresses I've ever owned, a dress that brings a shiver and a haunting sense of sadness even now. It was a white picoted organdy, made, I think, for a children's day program at Sunday School. I didn't quite understand, yet I knew there was a greater loss than my dress to me, when my kind father the next year when I was taller asked if I'd give the organdy to a little girl who needed it. I didn't know little Sarah well, but I'd heard about her and her lingering short life as a "blue baby." Now, surely she could be helped by medical science to grow up and play. Then, child of a family without much money and struggling to handle the medical expense, she needed my dress to wear as she joined the angels, and I'm glad still that I could give it to her.

3) (In this next piece the writer chose a different form in which to present her thoughts and memories—a poem. You will find more about this form in Chapter 7.)

Two Gray Dresses

Mother had a silken dress
Gray as many mornings when there is only a
    remnant of pink low on the horizon.
It was soft as gosling down.
I thought today how like the pussy willow
So smoothly gray and gently round.

With a pale rose at her throat
Mother's dress was Sunday best
*   and she wore it many years.*

The pussy willow wears her gray dress
Only until she stretches toward the sun
And bursts into yellow leafy bloom.

How extravagant!

One Memory Leads to Another

Herb entertained a writing class with a paper triggered by recalling three telephone numbers. The numbers brought back his experience as call-boy for the Soo Line.

An Essay on Memory

Funny thing about memory. The most insignificant things sometimes keep clear and bright, while the important things fade away.

I am reminded of years ago. In 1925 when I came to Stevens Point I got a job on the Soo Line. Most of the brakemen and just about all of the switchmen were single. Some of them lived in the old hotels on the South Side. There were three of them: the Majestic, the Dewey, and Worzalla's. Worzalla's was where Schierl Heating is now. There were a number of rooming houses also. Mrs. King's on the southeast corner of Dixon and Reserve, and Mrs. Feit's on Elk Street between Park Street and Shaurette were two of them.

I was a call-boy at the yard-office. The job consisted of walking around and calling the crews for the various switch-engines and trains.

I remember one night walking into Mrs. Feit's and upstairs on my way to get "Jump River Tom" for a train going out at about 3 a.m. The procedure was to open the bedroom door, reach up for the string in the middle of the room, which was tied to the light, jerk the covers off Tom, and slap him on the butt. All this in one continuous motion.

Well, this time I was greeted with a shriek, and here on this hot night I had a naked girl, scared to death. When the commotion died down and the apologies and explanations over, it seems that Tom had gone away for the week. Mrs. Feit's niece was visiting her. So what was more natural than to use the vacant bedroom?

But what I started out to say was, what trivia clutters up the mind! I called lots of my men at three whorehouses that existed on the east end of Patch Street. It seemed that they were the favorite R and R spots for these single switchmen and brakemen.

And after 50 years I can still remember the "White House" whose madam was Violet, the "Brown House" whose madam was Betty, and the "Tar-Paper Shack" whose madam was Gladys, better known as "Happy Bottom."

Well, that's trivia enough, but how about this: the telephone number for the White House was 34; for the Tar-Paper Shack, 342, and for the Brown House, 588.

When the laughter died down—and it took quite a while—Marge said, "Oh, my! That reminds me of my grandfather's car. I haven't thought of it in years." The following week the class understood the connection when Marge read them her story.

Grandfather Buys Another Car

When I answered the phone my grandmother's clipped "Let me speak to your mother" telegraphed a problem. Summoned, Mother listened without comment. Finally my grandmother paused long enough for Mother to interject a quick "What is he thinking of?" Grandmother continued and Mother was silent except for an occasional "I don't blame you" or "What ails him!" The conversation ended with Mother's stern comment, "He needn't expect any sympathy when he gets here."

It was apparent to me that my grandparents had suffered a difference of opinion and that my grandmother had sought and found an ally. In response to my unspoken question, Mother revealed that my grandfather had bought a used car.

He had a proclivity for them—especially black, seven-passenger models. In the 1930's he used them in his funeral work. Another should not have upset my grandmother. Before I could learn why this one had, my grandfather pulled into the driveway.

Mother was out the door and down the steps as the car stopped. Her first words, "You aren't going to buy that car," were uttered in disbelief. His answer was that it was bought and paid for. That left, he thought, no room for argument.

"Dad, you can't! You know whose car that was. Everyone in town will recognize it," countered my mother.

Grandfather was adamant. He had purchased it because he needed another funeral car and the price was right.

Then Mother played her trump card. Looking her father straight in the eye, right arm extended with index finger pointing, she proclaimed, "You may keep that car but I can tell you I will never let my children ride in it. I'll see that Willis doesn't let

Jim. When Midge gets here you can bet her children won't either."

That outburst ended the confrontation. Red-faced, with pipe clenched between his teeth, my grandfather stalked back to the car and roared out of the drive.

Peace reigned the next day. A brand new car replaced the offensive one. We never knew if Mother's ultimatum was the deciding factor. He may have decided that the car's image was too tarnished for funeral use. After all, its former owner was a prominent madam of a Patch Street house. And grandfather prided himself on his image as a very proper and dignified funeral director.

Both these pieces recount, through adult eyes, what transpired years before. They are dissimilar, though, in focus and structure. Herb recreates an earlier time by recalling, fifty years later, specific names and places and details, surprising himself almost as much as he impresses his readers. He elects (by choice? by chance?) to report his call-boy responsibilities and experiences matter-of-factly, without passing judgment on the antics of the adults he deals with. Marge remembers a forgotten episode, limits her narrative to that one incident, and enlivens it with realistic dialogue.

But the ripple-in-the-pond effect needn't stop with grandfather's car. What do these memories trigger for you? What telephone numbers come to mind from those days of few digits? What names and places? Perhaps you will recall and want to reflect on one of these:

- a family car feud
- a shady district
- an adolescent's (boy or girl) "rite of passage"
- a battle of the sexes
- a "you aren't going to buy *that*" argument

Moving Memories

The over-65's, experts tell us, are the most moving generation in the country. We retire from wintry climes and settle in
the sunny south—snowbirds fleeing from the snow. We weary
of the sameness of the seasons and return to the snow shovels.
We auction off or garage sale or give the children what we
don't want, pack the rest into a motor home, and relax in the
best of both worlds: Guadalajara in winter, Thousand Islands
in summer.

Well, we should be great movers. We've been doing it all
our lives. Write about a moving memory. Questions are often
a good way to help get started. Try some of these. Add some of
your own.

- How many houses/apartments have you lived in?
- What was it like to find them, furnish them, leave them?
- Did you ever return to a former home now inhabited by
  someone else? Did you feel, like Thomas Wolfe, that
  "you can't go home again"?
- What about the trail of sandboxes and herb gardens
  and bookshelves and neighbors you left across the
  country, even across the world?
- What about the lake cottage where the children learned
  to ski?
- What about the old house you rented furnished, complete with bats?
- What about your packing, transporting, unpacking
  experiences? Don't you deserve a medal by now?

More Memories

Sometimes memory pieces are more than just reveries.
Often, in a reflective mood, we like to use the past to make
a point about the present. We cite the days when there were
no income taxes or national debt—and still the country

prospered. We decry today's planned obsolescence and long for a toaster, a car, a lawn mower that lasts. We worry about the lassitude of the younger generation, wish they were upstanding citizens and workers—like us, of course.

Moments of discontent, as well as moments of pleasure, trigger reactions which we want to share. Our conclusions need airing, our convictions deserve a hearing. The result? A persuasive essay or letter or speech. In "Back to the Basics—Again," William F. Steuber questions recent educational trends and uses history to support his premise.

Back to the Basics—Again

Parents and educators for several years have been doubting the effectiveness, the wisdom and even the sanity of what has been promoted as progressive education. Overwhelming evidence has been gathered through surveys of entering college freshmen that too many Johnies and Janes can't read, write or do fractions. This past summer UW officials and faculty argued over whether the University should bear the financial burden of initiating remedial classes for these freshmen. Nationwide, parents and employers expecting competence in youth looking for work are angry. They are demanding that schools, indeed, go back to the basics.

What then are the basics?

It's generally accepted that the basics are reading, writing and arithmetic, taught by a competent teacher with a genuine love for her subject and her students to inspire the necessary self-discipline that makes learning a pleasure. After that there will be plenty of time to go on to nature, ecology, social studies, art, self-expression and all the other meaningful relationships.

The idea of stress on the basics is so old, and for a long dark period was so forgotten, that it is new all over again.

In Wisconsin in the opening years of this century, long before there were busses to bring country children into city and village schools, there were more than 6,200 rural school houses serving 170,000 farm and crossroads youngsters. Although the average school had 27 pupils there were nearly 50 schools with five or fewer; nevertheless a full-time teacher had to be available for each of the 6200 country schools.

Teachers graduating from the universities, colleges and normal schools were eagerly sought for the city schools. There were very few graduates available for country schools. Most rural school boards, working through their county superintendent of schools, had to look among qualified high school graduates, some as young as 15 or 16, for their teachers.

This was not so casual as it sounds, for these expectant teachers, fresh out of high school, had to survive an examination process that for its purpose was as selective as the professional boards are today for physicians, dentists, architects and engineers.

Basics? You bet. Here and there a set of these early teacher exams still exists, but they are rare. I have a set from the files of my late brother Milton, who took the exam in Baraboo at the age of 17 in the fall of 1906. He passed it, got his school, and a salary of $32 monthly for nine months, out of which he paid two dollars weekly for room and board. After he signed the contract the school board added, "Oh, and one more thing. The parents expect you to teach an hour of German each day."

The examination he took to get his teacher's certificate was in seven categories: algebra, geometry, English composition, American literature, English literature, physics and physical geography.

Automatically, the examination tested reading, comprehension, spelling and writing, those worrisome fundamentals to modern education. Competent arithmetic was assured through passing algebra and geometry parts.

To get his or her contract, the aspiring teacher had to make a high mark. There were no built-in helps to the examination. There were no true-false choices where simple luck gives a 50-50 chance. There were no multiple choices to aid the memory or nudge the logical faculty toward the proper answer resting fully visible as one of the provided choices. The answers reflected fully and only the applicant's competence.

The county school superintendents of those earlier days who graded the papers were severe. None of this averaging, or above-or-below-median juggling. It was a system that produced results. Hundreds of thousands of later successes in every walk of life came out of those rural one-room schools, taught by teachers who had learned their basics and survived their tests.

Now that high school minimum competency tests are beginning to catch on, tests asking students to perform such difficult tasks as to fill out a job application form, read a map, and balance a checkbook, it may be instructive to take a look at teacher examinations of 70 some years ago.

Do you agree with Steuber that education has deteriorated? Are we, as the blue ribbon panels claim, "a nation at risk"? Write a persuasive essay on this topic or another of your choice. Test your power of persuasion by sharing your writing with a friend or friendly group.

In the next essay Henry Butler reacted to the trigger of a classified ad. Like Butler, you can find ideas in anything, anywhere.

Seems to Me

For Sale: One collection of old-fashioned manners and courtesies. Present owner will consider any offer.

Unwilling as I may be to part with it, my polite upbringing by a strict New England father and a gracious southern mother is becoming a nuisance—no, a burden. I rise when a lady or a senior enters or leaves the room or stops to talk to me in a restaurant; I offer my seat on a train or a trolley to women, the elderly, and the weary; I open car doors, house doors, even barn doors for anything in skirts; and I say "ma'am" and "sir" when addressing anyone I do not know on a first-name basis. Very Edwardian, possibly "quaint," and apparently superfluous. Breezy bad manners seem to be the order of the day; I think both men and women consider it natural and macho. I've learned to live with the tolerant smiles I provoke, but I find the hostility I generate very uncomfortable.

The last time I offered my seat on the subway to a lady, she snarled, "What? What do you want?"

"Would you like to sit down?" I asked politely.

She backed away. "What for? Don't get smart with me."

I exited at the next stop, miles from my destination. The spirit of my mother wasn't going to allow me to sit while that lady was standing. If I try to change, a small army of gentle ghosts will constantly prompt me to mind my manners.

With "sir" and "ma'am" I produce everything from giggles to glares. "Don't call me that. It makes me feel old." Which isn't my intention. If I don't know someone's name, I try to be polite about it. Is "hey, mister" or "you, lady" a better choice? Some years ago in London, my tongue really tripped me. Auditioning young actresses, a painful process on both sides, I tried to lessen the awkwardness by ending each interview with, "I appreciate your coming in. Thank you . . . thank you, ma'am . . ." Most of the girls snickered, several blushed, some even stumbled over furniture on their way out. I asked my English colleague if I was doing something wrong.

"Not at all, dear boy," he said. "It's rather charming, but the 'ma'am' does put them off a bit. Over here, we only say that to the queen."

It hadn't occurred to me. Besides, I don't plan that kind of behavior in advance. It simply happens: The knees pull me to my feet, the hand goes for the door, and the "sir" and "ma'am" drop naturally into my conversation.

Those habits are difficult to break, and it occurs to me that I may not be ready to give them up. I keep remembering a scene from a favorite Louis Auchincloss novel, Portrait in Brownstone, *and an older woman saying, "Yes, young man, being polite is an effort, tiresome at times. But good manners is the only rag between us and the apes. Let's keep it there."*

Now, she and I know that it is not a life-or-death issue if I choose to walk on the curb side while escorting a lady on the street. (Legend says I am protecting her from mud splashes from carriage

*wheels.) Nor will planets collide if I fail to seat a
lady first in a restaurant. (Nowadays I may have to
fight her for the chair.) And the problems of pollu-
tion, nuclear freeze, and world hunger are not
solved by my allowing women, children, and my
elders to precede me on a bus, on and off an elevator, or into the lifeboats of a sinking ship. But
whether we're playing golf, shooting pool, dining
out, drowning, or sitting at a world conference,
everything seems to go more smoothly if we have a
set of rules to follow. I always find them useful for
ballroom dancing. And I appreciate anyone who is
polite to me, from the tax man who earnestly tries
to keep me out of jail to the driver who holds up for
10 seconds to let me fall, gasping, into the bus. The
mannerism is called "gallantry," with a deprecating
smile. The principle is called "deference," putting
the other fellow first. It often leads to tolerance,
understanding, and peace. And it costs nothing.*

*As mother used to say, "Dear, it's quite easy.
Just treat everyone the way you would like to be
treated." I think she read that somewhere.*

Pointers for Writing
Little Memories

Select

- the unforgettable. The unique or the universal may
  both be memorable; tell something that happened only
  to you or something from your experience that you feel
  sure is shared by others.
- an event with a memorable twist, an irony.
- a happening (experience) with a special (lingering)
  meaning.
- a milestone, either a stepping stone or a reversal.

- a person or relationship that stands out (haunting, awe-inspiring, loving, teaching).

Focus

- center on a single event, personality, scene. Like a good photograph,the little memory should be single in effect.
- tell all that is necessary, important.
- avoid the extraneous or excess; do not wander. Memorable events are likely to remind you of others; save the second memory for another writing.

Build

- arrange carefully to keep interest.
- save the punch (the point) for last, usually.
- lead the reader with you through a happening; be concerned with sequence.
- allow meaning to unfold; let it linger at the end; avoid the obvious of too much telling.

Picture

- choose details and facts to make scenes, persons, and events vivid. Looking—remembering—closely allows you to conjure up those details, to bring them to life again.
- find sharp, exact words that create images.
- use metaphor, simile, analogy to show what something or someone was "like" and share that likeness with your reader.

You'll find outlets for well-told memories, and if you start putting them together, you'll soon have a memoir.

Chapter 7

Writing Memoirs

"*Growing up with my Irish grandpops was a daily adventure . . . .*"

"*My very first memory is of being bitten by Rex, the neighbors' supposedly friendly old collie . . . .*"

$\mathscr{A}$ s soon as you read these sentences, you realize that you are reading a "life"—someone's memoirs. And even though you've never thought of writing an autobiography, it is a short step from recounting short memories to expanding those memories into a life story. Everyone's life is material for autobiography. You don't have to live in far countries, do anything earthshaking, or consort with famous persons to have the kind of experiences that make interesting reading. Nor does it matter whether you, only your family, or the world will read what you write.

Telling your own story is not hard. By collecting short memories, or perhaps by looking back and surveying all that has happened, you can organize your life into a sustained piece. After looking at your "life and times," it is a short step to extending your personal story into a family history.

So memoirs and family history, the subjects of these next chapters, intertwine. In looking at yourself, you will look back;

and in looking back, you'll be looking ahead. And here are some ways to do it.

Listing

Earlier we talked about using lists as starters. Ray, in an informal senior center class, decided to do a variation on listing. He chose one item for each year he was old, but he could have made the list thirty items or a hundred, any number since he didn't try to make the arrangement chronological. Here is Ray's introduction to his list and eighteen randomly selected from among his sixty-six "life" items.

By the Numbers

It has been said that as one begins to "hang it up," "pull the pin," or "ring the last bell"—that the number of years lived be used, and a situation one wishes to remember or have others remember be listed for each number. This is something I can do as an ex-biology instructor—list known facts. So here goes. I'll embellish these facts in later writings, I hope.

1. *I spoiled my mother's expectations of a Sunday chicken and dumplings dinner the day I was born. The doctor ate it. The worst blizzard of the year came that day with me.*
2. *I made my family very happy when I got my first college degree.*
3. *I married a great Norwegian girl, and became the father of a son.*
5. *We acquired a lovely, talented, etc. etc. daughter-in-law.*
6. *Thence on to a granddaughter and grandson about whom there are not enough complimentary adjectives.*

7. *Survived a massive cancer operation and the follow-up therapy. Now over!*

20. *Had more than 9,000 students in my classes, also 191 cadet teachers.*

26. *Was the last Master of the Plover Masonic Lodge #73. My Great Great Grandfather was its first chaplain over 125 years ago.*

28. *Collected 180 cowbells.*

33. *Fell into a trout stream three times last summer.*

39. *Flew close to Mount Everest. Just a hitchhike ride with no parachutes.*

40. *Climbed a minaret of the Taj Mahal in Agra, India.*

44. *Hunted barking deer at the base of the Himalaya Mountains. Our group got two. The natives sold them to a camel caravan trader for the makings of French perfume.*

50. *Was seasick all of the 58 days on the Pacific Ocean excepting while in port.*

58. *Liked, even enjoyed, high school sophomores (no one else seems to, not even their parents).*

60. *Was the only person the Baptist preacher dropped in the baptismal tub.*

65. *I plan on catching many trout this year and not falling in.*

66. *Saw an exceptional riptide on the Hoogly River. Jute flats tossed like matches.*

From these selected entries, you can see that Ray did not attempt to keep his list in chronological order. Nor was he concerned at this point with making detailed entries. Instead, with free association at play, he jotted down kernels of memories as they came to him.

When he looked over his full list and realized that 24 of the

66 items dealt with his World War II experiences overseas, he had found a starting point. His next writing centered on some of those adventures. In the list, Ray had the possibility for a longer memoir, and he could decide on inclusions, exclusions, and additions later.

Such random listing is a good first step to a memoir. When later you organize the free associations, you may choose a sequential pattern by beginning with the year of your birth, by dividing according to decades or by stages in your life.

Clustering

Maria started in another way to gather her ideas and focus her writing. Here she describes the process.

> It was the start of our Monday writing class, time for our usual ten-minute warmup. Eileen was responsible for the stimulus that day. "The subject is grandparents," she announced. And we all began to think and write.
>
> Ten minutes later—well, maybe fifteen—we put down our pens and, taking turns, read our products aloud, commenting on them ourselves, then listening to the reactions and suggestions of others. Here was my scribbling for that day:
>
> > It was the first time I had seen my mother cry. A September day when I was eight or nine. I had come home from school and there she was, not in the kitchen, but way, way in front of the house, just sitting on the living room sofa and crying quietly. A telegram had brought news that her mother had died. But it was not until days later that a letter from Uncle Chris really told us the story. And it was

not until years later that I fully understood that day.

Uncle Chris was the bachelor uncle all children should have—tall, handsome, red-haired, devil-may-care. The kind that carried my brother and me high on each shoulder and raced us around the yard, the kind that took us to the Lion Store, just before Christmas, and let us oh and ah and want this doll and that truck—only to have all the toys we had drooled over appear later under the tree.

So when he decided to go to Greece for a visit, we were devastated. How could we get along with just parents for a year or two—that was forever! But go to Greece he did. He landed in Athens, then wired his mother in Sparta that he was on his way. Two days later he reached Sparta to discover his mother had died of a heart attack when she received word that after twenty-five years she would see her son again.

She didn't see him again. And I never met her. And the loss was great for us all.

As I read my scribbled notes aloud, I realized that I really was going in several directions—not just one—that as a matter of fact I had at least three focuses here and, of course, no one of them pursued fully. But all of them intrigued me. I could write about

my mother who rarely cried
my grandmother's dramatic death
my Uncle Chris as a character
his role (importance of "extended family") in my
    childhood
I knew I didn't like the maudlin ending I had

*tacked on to my piece, but I also knew that, using
stories I'd been told, I might write about the grandmother I missed knowing.*

*Later, looking at the impromptu piece at home, I
spread out the ideas in "turkey tracks" to see where
they were leading me.* [Turkey-tracking, so named
by an imaginative student, is a form of clustering or
grouping ideas, a neat way to generate information
and to help find resulting connections.] *I started
with "grandparents" in the center and then began
to break it down into parts, then to break down the
parts into subsequent parts:*

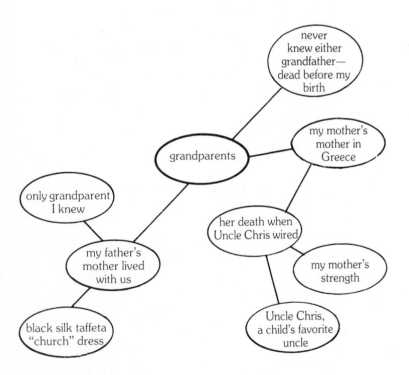

The clustering was working. I had included my original ideas, then left them to go on to add the other three grandparents. For the two grandfathers I had never known, there was nothing more to be said at this point. But, as I stared at my turkey tracks, memories of Grandmother K in her black taffeta dress came pouring into my mind: her Sunday dress that touched the toes of high-buttoned shoes, black of course; the jet black beads sewn on the collar; the tight, tiny waist; the wide-brimmed black straw hat worn straight—no rakish tilt for her. Yes, all these I could quickly add to the Sunday dress memory. But, for some reason, my mind left that entry dangling, too, and I found myself adding these entries instead:

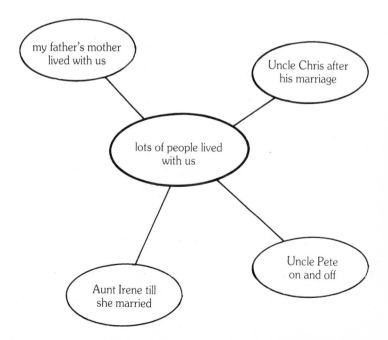

*The tracks were leading me in a new direction—
one that caught my interest: from Grandmother K,
to "lots of people lived with us," to naming some of
them, to the concept of my extended family and its
role in my life. Here was a connection to conjure
with! I needed much more thought and exploration,
but now I was aware of directions and possibilities.
What great projects I had at my fingertips and my
memory tips. I was ready to go beyond the track or
cluster and to fan out in a kind of chronology. My
next notes were:*

> *The early years*
>> *A grandparent, aunts, uncles, others live with
us for two weeks, two months, two years,
many years—there is always room and
welcome—till they marry, or find a job, or buy
a home, or . . .*

> *The teen years*
>> *Sundays the families gather at our house—six
adults, six children for dinner every week.
Senior by ten years, my brother and I "sit"
the others, then entertain them, escort them
to the park, to movies, to ball games, to
museums, to . . .*

> *The private years*
>> *We go to college, we get jobs, we move away,
we marry. We are busy with our own growing
families. Ties are not broken but they are
stretched.*

> *The later years*
>> *Our lives change, merge at the deaths of par-
ents, the marriages of children, the baptism of
grandchildren, the deaths of spouses. It is a
coming together—full circle. When we meet,
we are once again as we were as children—
close, caring, warm, accepting.*

In a circuitous fashion, Maria found stimulation and focus for her memories. Clustering is a simple and effective way to seek organization. And the fact that it is non-linear—you can shoot your ideas out in all directions all over the page—makes it even more versatile and inviting. "Through clustering," writes Gabriele Rico in *Writing the Natural Way*, "we naturally come up with a multitude of choices from a part of our mind where the experiences of a lifetime mill and mingle."

- Begin with a central word or phrase that interests you.
- With that in center page, branch out wherever ideas take you.
- Select among "branches" as a pattern emerges.

Using Thematic Triggers

Like the central word in Maria's cluster, any number of themes, central ideas, or even objects may set you thinking about the past and help you evolve an organization. You might proceed by choosing a trigger like one of these and then let it provoke memories and thoughts.

Houses and Towns
Go back to the "moving memories" from the last chapter. Now ask yourself some questions about all the places you have lived.
—What is the first home you remember? Can you still draw the floor plan? Sketch the surrounding area? Identify a favorite spot there?
—What memories do you have of other houses, apartments, mobile homes, cottages—any place that answered your need for "home"?
—And what about your hometown? What do you recall of times there? Have you returned in later years? What is it like through adult eyes?
—What of other cities and countries? Have you known any that had great impact on your life?

Jobs
—Remember your first job? In eighth grade? Dipping ice cream cones—two scoops for a nickel? Mowing lawns?
—And other jobs that followed—little ones and big ones—full time and part time—paying ones and volunteer ones, the ones you "caught" and the ones that "got away"?
—What about all the time you spent preparing— studying, apprenticing?
—Did you stay in your early career choice? What about promotions, transfers, changes?
—What were your greatest satisfactions? What decisions would you have made differently? Are you planning any career changes now?
—How about bosses and co-workers? Business for yourself? Unions? Forms in quadruplicate? TGIF?

Money
—Do you remember hot dogs or cigars for five cents? Rib roasts for twenty-two cents a pound, a Chrysler sedan for $995.00? (But who had the money?)
—How did you learn about money? Have you followed the advice of Polonius: "Neither a borrower nor a lender be"?

Conveyances
—What has been your experience from baby buggy to shank's mare to automobile to airplane?
—What's the story of your life "on the go"? Cars, boats, tricycles to ten-speeds, motorcycles, tractors, even spacecraft? Retiring to a motor home or boat that drops anchor almost anywhere?

Entertainments
—What did you do for fun? What do you recall about radio—Fibber McGee and his closet or

Gabriel Heater and his pronouncements?

—Trace your interests in sports—what you listened to, watched, thought about them. What's happened as TV came to dominate sports—how has time, money, spectatorship changed?

—Do your memories include the sweep from the silents to the talkies, from Ronald Coleman to Sylvester Stallone, from the twenty-five cent neighborhood movie to evening in front of the VCR?

—What about circuses and carnivals? Picnics and races? How have you "played" through the years?

School

—What were your dear old Golden Rule days like?

—How do your children's and grandchildren's school days compare to yours?

—When did you last attend a class? What was it? Did you ever attend a class reunion? How did you feel about it? And maybe Elderhostel?

Fashions and Fads

—Do styles today sometimes suggest a feeling of *deja vu*? Do you sometimes wish you had kept spike-heeled shoes or double-breasted suits for another time around?

—What other recycling intrigues you? The Big Band sound? Tap dancing? Convertible tops? Do things really change?

Music

—What about those music lessons? Recitals? Did your mother make you practice?

—How about lullabies you sang to the children? Were you in high school glee club or church choir? Band or operetta? A barber shop quartet? What music is part of your life now?

—What do your musical likes and dislikes tell about
you?
—What music do you associate with the big occasions in your life?

Add to this list of triggers on your own, and frame questions you can use to spark memories. Here are just a few more
suggestions:

Travel—from backpack to round the world flight
The natural world—activities and preservation
Fights—from misunderstandings to World War II
Jokes and language—in family talk, local speech, outside
world
Collections and other hobbies
Religion—its place in your life
Holidays and family traditions
Pets—cats, dogs, horses, or a zoo in the basement

This last one—pets—sparked memories and a focus for
Murilla, who wrote a short life history about the dogs that had
been "family." Here we have excerpted only connecting sentences from her "pet" memoir, but you can easily see how
she arrived at her title.

Dogs Who Have Owned Us

*Margaret of Dolyddelan is a Welsh terrier, the
last of a long succession of dogs we have owned, or,
more accurately, who have owned us. . . .*

As a child I had a mongrel named Perry. . . .

*When I married Ben, there was Jerry, a huge
hound. . . .*

Then there was Silver, a Samoyed. . . .

*Then there was Nellie, a placid American
Brown Spaniel . . .*

*When Nellie died . . . we could only have ano-
ther Brown, quite imaginatively called Brownie.*

> . . . He was replaced by a Chesapeake with fiery golden eyes. I didn't trust him. . . .
> Then there was Ranger, a Spaniel who had been criminally neglected. . . .
> During much of this time, we also lived with Ginger, a dog of mixed parentage. . . .
> Now we come to lovable Sparky, a beagle. . . . and his pen companion, Tippi, a magnificent Weimaraner. . . .
> After that came Pooka, whose real name was Baron von Frederick something or other, . . . a miniature Schnauzer. . . .
> And now there's Maggie. How often children decide what's best for parents! And so it was in this case. My children decided that a Welsh terrier would be an ideal home companion for me. . . .
> Ask me next year how we're doing.

In between these selected sentences, each of which signals the acquisition of a new dog, Murilla tells her pets' stories. And she reveals how each of them affected her life and her family. She begins and ends with the present, and in between she follows a chronological order—the usual controlling order for the body of a memoir.

Using Calendars and Other Dated Materials

Although you have probably moved many times and houses no longer have attics, most people carry around an accumulation of life records. These, like the other methods we've discussed, can spark the materials of memory.

> —Judy wanted to write the story of her years as a teacher in government schools abroad—two years in Saigon, four years in Heidelberg. She regretted not having kept a full diary of her experiences, but

remembered a "mess of stuff" she had boxed and saved. Within the box she found appointment calendars, travel vouchers, old plan books, programs, some pictures and slides, even a small collection of clippings. Hearing of the project, her sister and cousin dug up a few letters she had sent them. A motley bunch of stuff, but a gold mine of dated items provided pegs on which to hang her story. They brought back times and events dimly remembered or forgotten. Like Ray, she made lists and began to group some of the memories.

—Responding to repeated family requests, Mrs. Sharp attempted to put down a bit about her life. At 89, though, she had a hard time recalling things and keeping them in some kind of meaningful order. A friend suggested she lay out her family albums—use photographs of herself as a baby, as a girl, as a bride, and as a mother with children. The pictures brought the years into focus, helped her remember details and arrange them.

—When Jack retired from his accounting firm, he set aside morning hours to tackle a project he had long kept waiting—tracing his working life and his financial history. He had saved all the pertinent papers—job contracts, cancelled checks, bank statements, mortgages and loans, receipts, and income tax returns and records. Jack's painstaking efforts produced a detailed history of money management. Along with his own story came the story of his business and its reflection of national economic change.

As these examples show, dated materials serve to spark memories and ideas, as well as to help find an organizational pattern.

Responding to Ideas

Quotations often appear on the fly leaf or at the head of chapters in books of memoirs. One of those sensible or sardonic, wise or funny bits can serve as inspiration and provide a theme for your writing. As you glance through the following list, find one that touches you.

—*Life would be infinitely happier if we could only be born at the age of eighty and gradually approach eighteen.*

Mark Twain

—*Use it up, wear it out, make it do, or do without.*

Anonymous

—*To every thing there is a season, and a time to every purpose under the heaven.*

Ecclesiastes 3:1

—*The unexamined life is not worth living.*

Socrates

—*The first half of our life is ruined by our parents and the second half by our children.*

Clarence Darrow

—*Happy the man, and happy he alone,*
He who can call today his own;
He who, secure within, can say:
"Tomorrow, do thy worst, for I have lived today."

Horace

—*My grandfather always said that living is like licking honey off a thorn.*

Louis Adamic

—*"Are you married?"*
"Am I not a man? And is not a man stupid? So I married—wife, house, children, everything—the full catastrophe."

Zorba

—*One ought, every day at least, to hear a little song, read a*
good poem, see a fine picture, and, if it were possible, to
speak a few reasonable words.

Goethe

Does one of these quotations set you off? Adamic's sentence might, for instance, let you write about how life has presented you with many sweet things—but some of them proved hard getting! Or the one about "use it up" might lead to a memoir of depression days, and a pervading attitude that you carry because of that period.

Betty responded by developing a section which she later used in her longer memoir.

Saving String

These days I keep grocery bags lined up on the
workbench in the garage—one bag for aluminum
cans, one for "glass" glass, one for green glass, and
one for brown. And, yes, I stack the newspapers
and bundle them with twine when the pile gets a
foot or so high. None of this makes me a paragon of
virtue. Nor am I alone in what I do. For us depres-
sion kids, collecting and saving and recycling are
second nature. And in those years we weren't
thinking about ecology and disappearing resour-
ces. It was a question of survival.

Sheets which became worn and thin in the mid-
dle were cut in half and restitched, with the sturdier
edge sections becoming the new center. Worn out
towels were cut into small squares to serve as dish
rags, later still as dust cloths. Clothes were bought
or made with room to grow. My mother always
checked for generous seams and hems. Our out-
grown clothes reappeared on younger brothers
and sisters or even cousins or neighbors. Eventually

we'd nostalgically recognize some squares in the quilt grandmother was working on—pieces cut from favorite, favorite shirts or skirts.

Other habits were formed in those years, too. Coffee cans or piggy banks or bank accounts (when we could trust them again) needed donations "for a rainy day." And as for the "clean plate club"—well, there was no arguing there.

All such actions were a way of life. Planned obsolescence hadn't been invented yet. So I find myself annoyed with repairmen who tell me it's cheaper to replace than repair my dishwasher. Or, when my oven recently stopped functioning and I called the company only to be told patronizingly, "But, ma'am, ten or twelve years is the expected life of the stove."

Even if you don't think your autobiography is going to be important or widely read—even if you don't have a family pushing you to write it—remembering and ordering is worthwhile. Try anything that prods your memory and gets you started. Discover what your heart wants to tell.

Emily, a quilt collector in one of our writing groups, expressed her feeling this way:

From "Wedding Ring" to "Texas Star,"
From "Wind-blown Rose" to "Golden Gate";
From "Yankee Puzzle" to "Irish Chain,"
From "Postage Stamp" to "Dresden Plate"—

The patchwork pattern of my life
Becomes less crazy as I write.

Chapter 8

Writing Family History

"Did Grandma really ride a horse to school?" asks seven-year old Johnny. Just as children ask what it was like "back then," so do we. In this busy, transient world, almost everyone seems to be nostalgically interested in ancestral homes, historic sites, collectibles and family heirlooms; and many books and miniseries focus on stories of earlier days. Most of us, like Alex Haley, want to know more about our roots.

Writing family history is closely related to writing your personal memoirs, and a natural outgrowth. Or you may go at the two the other way around. Many of the techniques are the same. While your own story stems largely from inside yourself, family history involves more search and research. William J. Hofmann, who teaches a class of elder writers, comments on the rewards of writing family history.

> *Skeletons, saints, and a sense of self . . . Start writing family history, or what the Smithsonian likes to call family folklore, and you are likely to discover all three. The skeletons are rare and add a bit of spice. The saints are more common and*

closer to home than you would think. And between discovering family characters with their idiosyncrasies and admitting to a few of your own, you come finally to a better sense of who you are.

Family history is one of those broad generic terms which include genealogy, biography, autobiography, memoirs, and character sketches. It also includes letters, diaries, journals, reminiscences, and a variety of records from grade school report cards to presidential citations. Writing the family history means going beyond the genealogical record and the statistics to the discovery of personalities, adventures, family folklore, and the joys and sorrows of daily life. . . .

But there is more reward in writing family history and personal memoirs than simply leaving a record for someone else. There is the insight, the resolution of old conflicts, the paying of honor and tribute to those you've loved, and there is a new sense of self. For example, when I write about my own childhood, I suddenly grow more tolerant of my children. Remembering how my grandmother permitted me to melt crayons on her hot air furnace outlets makes me less critical of the Playdoh on the rec room floor. Remembering how my grandmother dismissed the vandalism of her fringed lamp shade each time I would pinch off a string of beads and carry them away for some project, I am shocked by my own willfulness and awed by the loving tolerance I enjoyed. Why my mother ever permitted me to keep poisonous snakes in the basement, or tolerated noxious fumes from my chemistry set, I'll never know, nor will I ever equal her patience and compassion. Such people are the saints in my family history. . . .

Nothing makes memory more vivid than writing about it. . . .

I cannot write of such moments without being made young again, and if there were no one to read it, there still would be reason to write it. . . .

Inevitably, family memoirs will encompass the times—give a picture of the environment, the ways people lived, the changing mores and ideals. In telling her story, Maude B. Rogers writes a history of change.

Changing Generations

This will not be a scholarly dissertation on generations, just ramblings about things I remember. I was born on July 4, 1894, so I span four generations. Life was rugged, there were few conveniences, but the people were sturdy and forceful. My husband's grandmother was such a person. They tell a story that Grandmother Rogers broke her parasol over the back of a woman who was lying drunk in the gutter in front of Mission Church in Boston. She then gave her a tongue lashing before she drove her off to Shanty Town. When Grandfather Rogers died, she divided her money amongst her four children and informed them that she would live with them as she chose, and did not expect to be invited formally but would come and go as she pleased. In those days grandparents, uncles, and aunts moved in with their children and relatives as a matter of course. Sometimes they were an asset, but more often they were a problem.

My parents' generation had more physical comforts although streets were not paved, streetcars were drawn by horses and heated in the winter by a stove in the middle of the car, stoked by the driver.

Later on, there were electric cars—open in the summer. You could ride to the end of the line for a nickel, a nice way to cool off on a hot summer's night.

At one time we lived in Cambridge and we loved to watch the Harvard boys speed by in their Red Devils (sports cars). I suppose they were going not more than fifteen miles an hour, but on football game days, children were kept off the street. We thought we were great when Dad hired a carryall and a pair of horses and we went for a Sunday gallop.

Housework was indeed a chore. Carpets were literally untacked once a year and beaten with a straw whisk. Washing was done on a washboard— first in moveable tubs which were also used for Saturday night baths, then later, in stationary tubs, such a joy because the water went down the drain and the tubs did not have to be emptied.

We lived in the city, so we could boast of an Archie Bunker "terlit" whereas my husband lived in the country and remembers their "Chick Sales," or outhouse. One hot summer day, his brother Everett and a pal had occasion to enter one, and another playful darling put a stick through the door handle, locking the boys inside. They feared suffocating or being eaten by the flies, so they took the only way out and fell in.

Mother's old friends, the Cronins, lived on a farm in Sutton. We often spent a Sunday with them, milking the cows and sloshing the pigs. Mrs. Cronin papered her "Chick Sales" with pictures of celebrities cut from the papers. On my next visit to the Cronin "Chick Sales" I gazed at Queen Marie of Romania, Eddie Rex, Prince of Wales, and there in the middle of them was I, Maude B, from my school newspaper announcing my lead part in the school play. From one throne to another.

By 1915 automobiles were more numerous, so one went on dates in style. I never understood then why my parents insisted I get home as soon as the play or game was over. Later on, I could not understand why my daughters, Sally Sue and twins Joan and Jane, could not get in earlier even though they explained that the "other girl" lived in West Seattle and had to be taken home first. Now the boys drive as far as Emunclaw or Mt. Vernon for dates. Distance lends enchantment.

It used to be that mothers and daughters were able to visit together while washing, ironing, and folding clothes. Now there is nothing to do but push the button and follow directions on all-temperature Cheer. Mother's generation wore corsets, corset covers, bloomers, petticoats, and featured high pompadour hair styles and sometimes lots of puffs. Our generation invented the bob and we wore combinations, a bit less confining than corsets. We wore bras and real silk stockings. My girls were daring and their generation eliminated all body-control gadgets, but did wear bras and went into shorts and socks. My grandchildren go braless, shoeless, and almost clothesless. They are absolutely honest in their belief—no inhibitions. They do not shy away from facts that we could not bring ourselves to face.

There have been many wonderful happenings in my lifetime such as Colonel Lindbergh's flight across the ocean, the United States putting the first man on the moon, and in my church, the eating of meat on Friday, ordination of laymen as Deacons, and perhaps soon, women ordained priests. I don't think we need to worry about the future. Our world

is in good hands with youngsters like our grand-
children. We think them brainless sometimes, but
they are compassionate and loving and my confi-
dence is strong in their ability to handle this world
when my generation is finished with its work.

Although Maude Rogers is writing from personal experience, her story offers a transition to consideration of family
history. She tells very little about herself—rather, she describes what it was like to live when and where she did. In her
essay, you'll notice characteristics common to family histories:

- She writes not just about herself, using an "I did this or
  that," but about "we," thus broadening her narrative to
  give a general picture.

- She gives a sense of moving through the generations,
  showing some of the changes that occur over the
  years—from Grandmother Rogers to her parents, to
  herself, her children and grandchildren.

- Although she can't include everything (no one can), she
  chooses significant details to mark each period:
  streetcars drawn by horses, carpets cleaned by beat-
  ing, Chick Sales, bobbed hair, Lingbergh's flight, men
  on the moon.
- She takes the approach of an observer-narrator who
  looks at events and puts them in perspective.

Finding Resources

All of these points are important to the potential family
historian. The techniques of listing and clustering, of organizing by themes or chronology, considered in the section on
memoirs, will serve in writing family history. Add to memory
the materials from your own research. Grab your notebook
and head for the library—or take a trip to far places where
your ancestors once lived—or prowl a cemetery for dates—or

write a dozen letters and get acquainted with distant cousins you never knew you had. They will probably welcome getting into the act. You'll undoubtedly get some real gems.

While a good newsy letter from a distant cousin is always a treat, a question-answer sheet often makes it easier for people to give you the information that you need. These suggestions will help you construct such a questionnaire.

- Lead off with questions asking individuals for factual information about themselves (name, date, residence, etc.) and then about parents, grandparents, and other family connections in their branch.

- Make or update a genealogical chart, and let the answers help fill in what you lack.

- Be sure to include questions asking for reminiscences and interesting tidbits which will become details in your story.

David James traced family history for several generations in his book *From Grand Mound to Scatter Creek*, a collection of memories about early Jameses who migrated from Cornwall to the Oregon Territory. The history begins with Samuel and Anna Maria James, who, with their eight children, traveled the Oregon Trail in 1850-51. James records the changes in their life as they left the social and agricultural situation of 1840's England and began anew.

Luckily, Samuel and Anna left documentation of their journey in diaries and letters. With further research, the author added topographic maps, sketches, and pictures of people, barns, houses and schools to illustrate life on the trail and in several frontier settlements. His pursuit of family history and genealogy has brought together many distant members of the family in a "Family Association" that now holds an annual reunion.

David James found time for his research and writing after he retired, just as Carolyn and Arnold Peterson are doing.

"We didn't have time before," they say, although they have had a lifelong interest in family beginnings and genealogy. Now they are attempting to pull together the history of his Swedish family, who settled in Minnesota, and her people, English farmers transplanted first to New England and then to Iowa and later to the Northwest.

Like David James, the Petersons have quite a collection of family papers—diaries, letters, records of property transactions, school reports, newspaper clippings, etc. Their research has led them to new interests—to exploring genealogical archives, travel to old homesteads, even to Scandinavia and England for dates and records and, Carolyn says, for "the atmosphere—a sense of where we came from."

"Finding some of the family always seems to bring another," says Carolyn. "We've even placed a few ads in the genealogy sections of magazines that run those things. A couple of these brought interesting answers and resulted in fascinating correspondence, even if we didn't turn out to be related. It all brings a lot of satisfaction, and besides, I think it is something our generation needs to do now. Certainly our children's generation hasn't the time, and with each decade the history becomes harder to unearth and piece together. If it's ever to be done, it's up to us."

Just as you often can benefit from sharing research, you may want to make a joint project of writing a family history. Marian Kanable and Jean Kanable Birkett did that in their book, *The Store (phone 306)*. They did their reminiscing and planning together, and each sister wrote a chapter turnabout. These paragraphs tell part of their family story a generation back:

> *Teaching in one-room rural schools was demanding work. The teacher taught all subjects to all eight grades. Many a person tells of incidents in the past that show Dad as fun-loving, considerate, and patient. But those stories do not come from his*

teaching years. Attendance might reach sixty pupils during the three month long winter term. It was most likely high enrollment and a bad day that resulted in the story that Dad had actually thrown a willful, defiant student clear across the school house.

The teacher, as janitor, also had to be responsible for keeping the stove going in winter, which leads to another story documenting Dad's starting the first hot lunch program in the area. He devised a way of banking the wood-burning stove in the school so that the students could bake potatoes which would be steamy hot just at the noon time break. That winter the hot potato lunch was quite a novelty, and Dad's fame spread around the Kickapoo.

In a rare story about his teaching career, Dad led out with the question, "Do you know how the Elk Creek School got its name?" Without waiting for an answer, he continued. "Way back in the 1850's, a herd of elk deer came down south as far as the edge of the creek. The winter was bad with more snow than usual. The herd tramped down the snow and stayed there the whole winter. The school gets its name by being on the spot where they stayed. Frank Fowell, our Hopewell neighbor, told me. I'll drive you girls by that school sometime."

Although Mother and Dad had grown up in the same general area of the Kickapoo River—Mother on Sylvan Ridge near the Hopewell Church and Dad in Kanable Hollow just east of Viola—the two families had only a nodding acquaintance. When he returned to the Kickapoo, Dad usually went to all the church socials and ball games. The Harn girls too loved a good time and attended picnics, dances, and games. Dad discovered that he and Mother had interests in education, dancing, and people in common.

In 1915, the National Guard was summoned to Texas for the Mexican Border incident. Mother left for Milwaukee to take courses so that she could teach high school English. Mother and Dad began a correspondence which would last through World War I. Mother saved the letters and even talked of reproducing them in a diary form as a memento for us, but the job appeared too great for one who never learned to type. When we were clearing out the attic after Mother died, we came to the packages of old letters tied with faded pinkish ribbon. We discussed the idea of reproducing Dad's letters. After thoughtful discussions, we decided that since Mother had not carried out her plan, there might be more reasons for leaving the letters between the lieutenant and his lady unread.

Dad returned to Texas, taught the winter term at Elk Creek and was commissioned First Lieutenant. He was soon on his way to France. He and mother had "an understanding" that if he returned home, they would be married. Dad was lucky. As an instructor of small arms, he had a relatively safe assignment behind the front lines in France.

"Tell us about the time you broke your leg in France riding your motorcycle," we used to beg. "No, tell us about the big house you were invited to where they served you wine in glasses as small as thimbles that was so strong that it almost knocked you down," or "Dad, tell us about your best birthday of all." That last request nearly always motivated Dad to tell us about how all the soldiers in his company waited and watched, hoping no one would be killed before the eleventh month of 1918, Armistice Day. The men all knew it was Dad's

birthday, and he said the celebration began cau-
tiously at 11:00 A.M. and continued, becoming
more and more ecstatic right down to the raucous
hours of the next day. The "war to end all wars"
was over, and peace had come. No subsequent
birthday was to hold so much meaning for Dad.

Reading this, you are immediately aware of how the writer uses detail and dialogue to make both the personality and past scenes come alive. The "hand-me-down" stories in any family become part of its history.

At times a family history is written by someone outside the family itself. Most of us know stories of the town's leading citizens, of early settlements, of romantic "real life" histories that could be told. Suzanne Hart O'Regan is such a history writer. Her book *Family Letters* follows the life of Theda A. Clark, from her birth in 1871 to death following childbirth in 1903. The story, however, is more than that. It is a social record—a picture of a wealthy family at the turn of the century, a history of their town, and of the Kimberly-Clark Corporation they founded.

O'Regan had the advantage of acquaintance with the place or places in her story and with persons who "knew how it was" or "knew somebody." She acknowledges conversations—oral history—and friendships with family descendants, the personal materials they supplied her, and the company records and memorabilia. Her book is enhanced by many reproductions of photographs and documents.

Coincidence or accident can sometimes lead to family history, just as genealogy and family reunions can provide impetus. Curiosity about an antique led Evalyn Attoe Blumer to an adventure in research, and to the writing of *To the Last Bird.* In 1946 she and her husband bought a cherry chest (circa 1785) from a man who called himself "the last Bird." It was an early serpentine chest of drawers which the owner claimed had been brought from New York by way of the Erie Canal. As she had the chest restored and discovered how rare it was, her curiosity prompted a search of over twenty years. She slowly uncovered the hundred sixty year history of the Bird family, from their origins in Vermont, to largely unsettled areas of New York, then on to the wilds of Wisconsin Territory.

A little chance and a lot of curiosity can lead you to discoveries about your family and others, and can become the best possible material for writing. With family stories, you almost always have a ready group of appreciative readers. But even more important is the personal enrichment that comes with such a project. Here is the way Marian Kanable and Jean Kanable Birkett said it:

> All of those years, the Store defined our world. It regulated our day, month, and year as surely as each season regulated the lives of our customers. The Store attracted our circles of friends, becoming the meeting place, the station along the way. When traveling relatives checked in at the store, Mother shifted into high gear to organize a "company" dinner at home in between doing bookwork, helping customers, and answering the phone. Even weddings and funerals had to be fitted into the schedule of the Store.
>
> Could the folks possibly know when they gave the Store its name, the significance of the Central Store?
>
> Writing this book has made us appreciate the wealth we have been given in place, people, and especially parents.

Part IV

Writing—
Forms
That Go
Public

Chapter 9

Writing about the Lives of Others

Biography and History

Everyone seems to like to "people-watch." Magazines and television programs—all media, in fact—constantly feature stories that both pique and satisfy our curiosity about the lives of others. Many best-selling books are biographies, sometimes of celebrities, the rich and famous, but often of rather obscure individuals who happen to catch a writer's attention.

Writing autobiographically leads naturally to writing about other people and the events of other lives and times of history. Perhaps you will never undertake anything as long as a definitive biography, a history of a period or some great event; but you can readily find outlets for biographical sketches and short histories. This kind of writing serves a purpose in many groups and communities.

Phoebe Smith, one of the founders of a very successful senior center, for some time wrote a column called "Senior Newsmakers." Her feature was a miniature biography of someone in the area covered by the circulation of the weekly newspaper where it appeared. More recently, Phoebe has turned some of the short biographies into longer ones and published a little volume entitled *80 Candles*. You can guess the emphasis from the title, for all the stories in the book trace very active and interesting lives now entering a ninth decade! Here is an example of one of Phoebe's "newsmaker" biographies:

Sharing Is What Verne Macdonnell Enjoys Most

She has a soft voice, a modest manner and a flitting twinkle in her eye. She appears to be a very quiet person. One would never guess Verne Macdonnell to be the effective busy individual that she is.

Her greatest satisfaction comes from giving a hand to any group or individual who needs her help. When asked why, she had a clear, well thought-out response. "Some people like the appreciation they get from the receiver. Some people like a pat on the back. Some have a desire to repay the world for the good they have received, and some hope that when they need help, they will get it. And then some people just enjoy sharing. I guess I'm motivated by all these feelings."

She must be, for her repertoire of service activities is large. For the last three years she has served as treasurer to the Bainbridge Foundation—a huge job. She has been treasurer to the Helpline House board and is currently treasurer of the Bainbridge Island Senior Citizens Center. But that's not all. She has been doing telephone reassurance for

BISCC and furnished emergency transportation for Helpline. She assists a school nurse with her book work and with weighing and measuring children in several schools and occasionally helps in one of their homes when the need is great.

But that's not all. Probably the most creative of her activities centers around the dolls she dresses and boxes for Christmas presents to be given to young clients of Helpline. At the moment she has 36 dolls and six stuffed animals ready.

This activity began five years ago when a family illness required her to quit work and stay home. She buys dolls at garage sales for about 50 cents. If parts are missing, she orders them from a company in New York. She washes, shampoos, paints and dresses each doll. Then a wardrobe is added, including a knitted coat and hat and a blanket or quilt. The doll is placed in an open box decorated with Christmas paper, and the box is covered with saran wrap. What a beautiful gift! She makes her own patterns, as no two dolls are the same. These dolls are a year 'round project, and one has but to see her living room display to realize how much she puts into it.

Verne came into the world earlier than expected while her mother was visiting a grandmother in Wisconsin. She was raised, finished high school, went to business college and was married in Lake Linden, Michigan. She worked three years in Chicago with bookkeeping machines, and eight years at the Argonne Laboratories of the Atomic Energy Commission in Lamont, Illinois.

Twenty years ago, her husband discovered the Northwest on a business trip and Bainbridge Island on an impulsive ferry ride. Don is a genetic engineer at the Fred Hutchinson Cancer Research Institute

> *in Seattle and likes his work so well, he can't visual-*
> *ize ever leaving it. They have a son on Bainbridge*
> *and a daughter who is a physical therapist in Santa*
> *Barbara. There are two grandchildren.*
>
> *Verne's philosophy became apparent when she*
> *said, "I feel there is too much unnecessary friction*
> *among people. We are on this earth such a short*
> *time, we should enjoy life and not spoil it for our-*
> *selves or others. We should do our best living today.*
> *Tomorrow is uncertain. Maybe we should each*
> *ask, 'How do I want to be remembered?' "*
>
> *Verne should have no problem answering that*
> *question.*

You will notice that Phoebe focuses on how her subject's activities represent her personality and philosophy. She wants to paint a picture of Verne by giving some of her major characteristics. Then in paragraphs 6 and 7, she lists briefly the factual information—birth, education, work, family, and so on—that we expect in biographies. Phoebe has the advantage of writing from direct knowledge, from knowing or interviewing the person. But consider how she creates the impression:

- What details does she choose to show the "sharing"? the"busyness"?
- What is the effect of quoting Verne directly?
- The author gives facts about Verne's life and her activities. What emphasis is achieved by the relative proportion of each?
- What is the effect of opening with a brief physical description? of ending with a bit of philosophy?

Similar short biographical sketches are found in many publications and have many uses. You might, for instance, write a short "bio" of each member of a club, of the officers in a company, of the candidates for offices in a professional organization, of old classmates checking up on each other at a time of a reunion, or of newcomers or new members to be presented to a group.

This interpretive or focused sketch is only one kind of short biography. At times you may have reason to write a very factual and straightforward account of someone's life, much like a report that you find in an encyclopedia. You probably have never heard of Elwood Haynes, but you will learn many facts about him from this *Americana* entry:

> **Haynes, Elwood** *(1847-1925), American automobile inventor and manufacturer. He was born in Portland, Ind., on Oct. 14, 1857, and graduated from Worcester Polytechnic Institute in 1881. As early as 1891, Haynes began work on developing an automobile, and he and the Apperson brothers, Elmer and Edgar, produced their first one-cylinder car on July 4, 1894. They formed the Haynes-Apperson Automobile Company in 1898, but after 10 years of manufacturing the Haynes-Apperson car, the partners separated in a dispute over credit for the design of the 1894 car.*
>
> *Haynes continued to manufacture his car at Kokomo, Ind., until the early 1920's. Although his automobile factory was the oldest in the United States, it was too small to survive in a period when the industry it had helped to found was undergoing spectacular growth.*
>
> *While Haynes' claim to have anticipated the Duryea brothers in the construction and operation of a successful gasoline automobile cannot be sustained, he was close behind them, and commercially his was far more successful. In 1901 the Apperson brothers drove one of his cars 1,050 miles (1,680 km) from Kokomo to New York in 73 hours running time, a remarkable achievement.*

Haynes also developed Stellite, a cobalt chro-
mium alloy used for making cutting tools. He died in
Kokomo, Ind., on April 13, 1925.

Robert S. Woodbury
Massachusetts Institute of Technology

Biographies, whether short or long, whether the sources are from first-hand acquaintance or unearthed only through research, may be written just to give information, or they may be written to interpret the subject's life, lending through imagination some insight into what things were like, how the person felt or thought, what certain events meant to the person living then or to others. We may distinguish between these types, calling the one a reporter's biography, the other an artist's. Both kinds have their places. The reporter must search for facts and report these carefully. The artist must decide how far to go in speculating or interpreting those facts. Writers in all cases must decide what to include, what to leave out.

Here are some things to think about as you write biographical sketches as a reporter:

- How much information shall I include?
- Which facts are pertinent for my purpose?
- Are my facts accurate? Are they verifiable?
- How shall I arrange the information? (For instance, shall I present straight chronology? Open with a list of achievements and then go back to show the early preparation, etc.?)

The artist in the same way begins by finding and weighing facts. But here there is a further consideration—how far can I go with speculation? How can I distinguish carefully so that the reader will accept my interpretation?

For instance, in writing her biography of Mary Boykin Chesnut, Elizabeth Muhlenfeld used diaries and letters for both facts and expressions of her subject's feelings. But Muhlenfeld goes beyond the sources to make statements like these: "It must have been with considerable anxiety, therefore, that Mary watched her nephew prepare for a duel" and "It is reasonable to assume that Mary Boykin Chesnut viewed these proceedings with profound disapproval."

When the biographer inserts her thoughts about her subject's possible thoughts, she is careful to choose words that let the reader know when these added bits are speculation or interpretation. Sometimes we accuse biographers of unfair slanting or bias; such care as Muhlenfeld takes is a way to avoid that accusation and still give the reader the advantage of the story element, the fascination that comes from reading an artistic and interpretive biography.

Of course, writers of both types—factual or interpretive—can slant their pictures. It does not follow that this is necessarily wrong, for you as writer can decide on the information and impression you want to give. You control the effect by the choice of what you put in, what you leave out. But bias should not lead to distortion. The truthful biographer guards against that. If your desire is to be factual and objective, that purpose will control what you do with your material. If you wish to interpret, to paint a portrait, your attitude and the impression you want to give of the subject will guide the way you write.

Enjoy the skills of Lisa Hammel, the author of this short biography of Fannie Farmer.

The Quintessential New Englander

When Fannie Farmer died 70 years ago, her name was a household word—literally. It adorned a cookbook that had already been a best seller for two decades. . . .

Her name, yes. But when she died, almost nothing was known of her life. . . .

Fannie Merritt Farmer was born in Boston on March 23, 1857, to John Franklin Farmer, a printer and editor, and Mary Watson (Merritt) Farmer, the eldest of their four daughters. She grew up in nearby Medford, eagerly planning a future that centered on going to college. But calamity shattered her plans while she was still a teenager. It is not clear whether she experienced a stroke or suffered an illness such as polio, but in any case, her left leg was affected and she walked with a pronounced limp.

Her doctors forbade a formal education. The world must have shrunk terrifyingly for her. What career would be possible without some sort of training? As to marriage, what hope was there for a somewhat plain and moderately circumstanced girl with a palpable disability?

Slowly she rallied, began to take on a share of the household duties, and became fascinated with cooking. When the family decided to take in boarders—Fannie was about 28 at the time—she found herself with a broader audience to please and seemed to thrive on it. It had become apparent that hers was no ordinary skill in the kitchen; those close to her urged her to train for a career teaching cooking. . . .

In 1887, when she was about 30, she entered the Boston Cooking School, already an institution of repute that had been started eight years before by the Women's Education Association of Boston. Mary Bailey Lincoln was the school's first principal.

Fannie's surprising energy, her practical experience, and her happy mix of logical and intuitive skills must have burst into flower in that congenial atmosphere. She had scarcely graduated in 1889 when she was asked to return as assistant to the principal, Carrie M. Dearborn. When Mrs. Dearborn died two years later, the board of trustees elevated Miss Farmer to the post. Her disability seems to have gone unnoticed.

Fannie's view that cooking should be as much a science as an art caught up early with the casual measurements of the time. Directions were then given in approximates: rounded teaspoons (any old teaspoon would do), heaping cups (use the cup of your choice, whatever its size), a walnut-sized lump of this, a dab of that, and so forth. There had been occasional faint mutters among professional cooks on the matter, but no one had thought to do much about it.

In an oft-told tale, it was said that Fannie was showing a youngster or youngsters something about cooking. A little girl, whose name in almost every version of the tale is Marcia, observes that the heaped teaspoon called for could turn out to be a different quantity each time. Miss Farmer is delighted with this bit of precocity and promptly invents the level measurement.

What is much more likely is that Fannie had been pondering the matter for some time and became even more confirmed in her determination to promote "scientific cookery" when she was asked to judge a recipe contest for a brand of flour and realized that of 800 entries, only about five percent used reliable level measurements. . . .

Her most famous book is The Boston Cooking School Cook Book, first published in 1896, and eventually to be known around the world simply as The Fannie Farmer Cookbook. It featured hundreds of clearly written recipes tested not only by the author but by students and faculty, and it was crammed with brisk information, chemical expositions, culinary physics, the physiology of flesh and fish, how-tos and ways-of, charts and tables,

household hints, lists of menus, and at the end a
prospectus of the cooking school's offerings. She
took it to Boston's most respectable publishers,
Little, Brown and Company. When, with a degree
of shortsightedness rare in the annals of publishing,
they turned her down, she persuaded them to bring
out 3,000 copies by agreeing to pay for the printing.
It became one of the all-time best-sellers, went
through 12 revisions, innumerable printings, and in
a very altered form is still in print today. . . . The
book is the center of Fannie Farmer. That richly
complex woman is reflected in its variety, its clarity,
its breadth, its stern passion, and the strength of
character that underlies it like New England
granite. . . .

Fannie wrote the right book for the right time.
With no apology and no coddling, she ran her read-
ers through masses of scientific and semi-scientific
data. She gave them a sense of dignity in their work
at a time when women were straining in their old
roles. But she also offered them reassuring,
unequivocal authority.

In 1902, after 11 years as principal of the Boston
Cooking School, Fannie decided to strike out on
her own and opened Miss Farmer's School of
Cookery on Huntington Avenue. The success of
her book provided the financing, and she was now
able to emphasize her interest in teaching individu-
als to cook rather than teaching how to teach.

She not only ran the school, with a faculty of five
(and five maids), but she also had other balls in the
air. She reached a wide audience with her monthly
food columns in the Woman's Home Companion,
written from 1905 to 1915 with help from her sister,
Cora Farmer Perkins. All during this time Fannie
was turning out other books, although none of

them had the success and fame of her first. Among them was one published in 1904 called Food and Cookery for the Sick and Convalescent, a subject that understandably interested her. She liked to say that this was her most important work. Her schools offered courses in cooking for the ill, and she once gave a series of lectures at the Harvard Medical School on the subject.

But she was better known for her popular lecture demonstrations given twice every Wednesday at the school. In the morning she addressed housewives, in the evening professional cooks. She also spoke to women's organizations and other groups, her tours taking her as far as the West Coast.

Often dressed in white, which must have effectively set off her red hair, and with her blue eyes even more intense behind rimless pince-nez, she would talk her way through a formidable array of dishes, some of which she worked on herself, some done with assistance. Her shyness seemed to disappear on the platform, and the talks were frequently reported in the Boston Transcript, alongside columns crowded with reports of activities of that ubiquitous phenomenon of the late 19th century, the uplifting women's clubs.

Her belief in the critical importance of nutrition to health, well-being, and the betterment of the human race was central to her writing and teaching. Its handmaiden was careful cookery. In a motto worthy of being needlepointed and hung on every kitchen wall, she said: "Progress in civilization has been accompanied by progress in cookery." Elsewhere in her cookbook she wrote, "scientific cookery . . . means the elevation of the human race." . . .

She would rush off to restaurants in Boston or New York when given word that there was a superior dish being served upon which she had not dined, and many were the lace-edged handkerchiefs that came home holding samples. Or if she encountered a sauce she could not identify, she would dab a bit on a calling card and fold it securely for transportation to the school kitchens where she, the faculty, and students plumbed the depths of the mystery.

Fannie eventually suffered a stroke, probably in 1908, that left her totally without the use of her legs. She was to spend the remaining seven years of her life alternating between crutches and a wheelchair. She may also have had an additional unnamed illness which could have led to her death.

Her response to this depressing and overwhelming threat was to live wisely and carefully and gloriously in spite of it. She continued to run the school, turn out books, write her columns, and give her lectures, the last only ten days before she died.

She died on January 15, 1915. The Woman's Home Companion *couldn't bring itself to give the bad news to its readers and ran her columns for the next 11 months without mentioning that they were posthumous. Fannie's last column contained many of the staunch New England dishes that had come to be associated with her. Among them were Boston baked beans, steamed brown bread, baked and stuffed haddock, Indian pudding, and salt codfish balls. It was a fitting farewell.*

- Be sure you notice—

Hammel's thorough research
The way she uses dates and time sequence

The way she creates physical impression—e.g., "Often dressed in white "

The way she conveys personality—e.g., "Fannie's surprising energy . . . her happy mix of logical and intuitive skills"

The breadth of detail, facts and impressions from many areas

The repeated emphasis upon Farmer's representation of New England characteristics

Her use of quotation and anecdote

Doing the Research

In a sense a biography is a history of a person, and writing a biographical sketch such as Hammel's and writing a short historical sketch are similar. Certainly the same types of source materials are useful in writing both. Many of these are identified in the section on memoirs and family history. They fall into two broad areas:

Primary information comes from knowing the subject (locale or area, events, etc.) first hand; from acquaintance or interview; from persons who had such acquaintance; from the writings, speeches, diaries, letters, etc. of the person whose story (people whose history) you are telling.

Secondary information comes from a step farther off. Writing without personal acquaintance with your subject, or having his or her personal papers, etc., involves the use of what others have written. Research about persons and events back in time comes from secondary materials. In dealing with these, you haunt libraries, read, and take notes.

With both primary and secondary materials, you will want to look at all sides of issues or controversies. For instance, if two people tell or write from differing viewpoints (one obviously likes your subject, another criticizes), you eventually must weigh the information and decide what to do with it: report one, support another, toss both out and seek additonal information, or what?

Research—whether you use primary or secondary sources—takes time, but part of the fun is in the digging, as you surely sensed if you tried writing a memoir or family story. Barbara Tuchman, who writes both history and biography, warns in her essay "In Search of History" that the researcher must know when to quit. Even if you have no deadline pushing you, her advice is good. You, too, want the eventual satisfaction of seeing what you can make out of all the materials you discover and assemble.

As with biographical sketches, you can find many purposes and outlets for short historical essays. Some of the illustrations and suggestions that follow should give you ideas and help you discover some of the techniques that make such writing worthwhile and the reading a pleasure.

Often a centennial or other anniversary makes us aware of historical events that we've previously given little thought. L. F. Willard, a contributing editor on *Yankee* magazine, succeeds in doing just that.

A Highway Heads for Fifty

In 1940 I was an up-country New Englander on my way to New York City, the glittering metropolis I had dreamed about but never visited. I figured I was getting close when I hit the Merritt Parkway south of New Haven. It was a revelation, a four-lane divided highway on which you could pass a car on a hill or curve—of which there were plenty—and not chance being clobbered by a car coming the other way. To a Vermonter, this highway seemed a brilliant solution to a natural problem. It never occurred to me that one day engineers would just level the hills, shovel them out of the way, making the roads so level, straight, and dull, that drivers would fall asleep out of sheer boredom. That can't happen on the Merritt Parkway.

Like a lot of people who travel that parkway with some frequency, I have adopted a protective attitude toward it. At the age of 50, it is aging gracefully. The saplings planted in the esplanade have reached maturity, often touching branches with trees on the other side, creating occasional green tunnels. Ivy has grown out along the stone arches of many of the overpasses, and some of these bridges seem to come out of the treetops, cross the highway, and disappear into the treetops again.

Many of the bridges—there are 36 of them—have the look of a Roman aqueduct. Their designer, George Dunkelberger, introduced a variety of playful design elements into the bridges, no two of which are alike. Built to resemble English or Italian bridges, or with an unmistakable art deco motif, some bridges have a single arch, and some dip down to the esplanade and bounce to the other side on double arches. Grapevines, spider webs, and geometrical designs have been incorporated into the decorative iron work of the railings, and an occasional stone sculpture stands guard where it hasn't been covered over with ivy.

Probably most appreciated by those who travel this road is the absence of buildings or other signs of civilization along almost all of its 37.5-mile length from the Housatonic River bridge to the New York border. What you see are trees, shrubs, wildflowers, and in the spring, the blossoms of dogwood and mountain laurel. The fall foliage is as spectacular as almost anywhere in New England. This shroud of

*urban wilderness came about because the state
bought twice as much land as was needed along the
route to allow for future expansion which, as yet,
seems doubtful, for a while anyway. The people of
Fairfield County like the Merritt Parkway as it is,
warts and all.*

*I drive the Merritt Parkway whenever I travel
south. What this route was for me on that day in
1940 when I first drove along it, it can never be
again: my own royal road to romance, the gateway
to adventure, to sights unseen. It is now a road that
gets me from here to there, but still, it's a passage
more pleasant than most.*

Willard maintains the careful sequence of practically all
biographical-historical writing, and he offers statistics discovered by research. Like other historians, he asks not only *what*
happened but *why*. The way he interweaves facts with his
experience in driving the Parkway and interjects his admitted
bias—his liking for the road that some people might think
obsolete—makes his writing lively and personal.

Try Your Hand

The opportunities for writing short biographies or histories
are limitless. Here are some projects for which you will have an
outlet among a circle of friends, in organizations to which you
belong, in your community. Many of them can easily lead to
something publishable. You may want to start with the suggestions here or find others of your own.

Group I—presenting personalities

1. *Who's Who* includes the names of persons who have
achieved something that is of "reference interest." Nominate
someone you think should be included (whether the name is

already there makes no difference), and write the notice that should go under the name.

2. Write a sketch of one of these persons who has been especially helpful to you:
    —a favorite teacher
    —a pastor, rabbi, priest or other religious leader of influence
    —a doctor, dentist, other health care worker
    —a salesperson, mechanic, janitor, other person in a service occupation

3. Write a personality sketch about one of your relatives: the one you like most, the most colorful, the one you would like to disown , etc. If you wish, try an unusual format like that pictured here:

WORDS
FOR A GRANDFATHER SAMPLER

Founder
Puritan
Indian Captive
Minister—Minute Man—Miller
Blacksmith—Patriot—Cooper
Indian Fighter
Postmaster
Mason
Erie Canaller—Stage Liner
Whaler—Hotel Keeper—Farmer
Yankee Peddler & Pinery Logger

Grandfathers All—Americans All
1637-1946

mfw
1982

4. Write a short sketch of some celebrity you watch on television or know through other entertainment. Do whatever research you think necessary to make your sketch factual as well as interesting.

5. Write an introduction for one of these persons you think your readers should know (you, of course, determine the readers):

—a new neighbor
—new employee, new member of a business staff
—a new member of an executive board or committee
—a newly elected official in some office
—a new member of a club, lodge, some other group to which you belong

6. Imaginary meetings with famous persons from the past have been the subject for books, plays and stories. Choose some figure from history whom you would most like to have known, or with whom you would like to have a conversation. Write a biographical sketch about the person. If you want, present it in dialogue and let the interviewee speak about his or her own life. For instance, you might ask James Monroe about current relationships with Latin American countries. Or imagine a conversation between Queen Victoria and the Lady Di, the Princess of Wales.

Group II—writing about past events

1. Almost all types of institutions are subjects for history writing. Often such records are published for special groups or for special occasions—for instance, the history of a school at the time of a reunion or anniversary. Write a history of an institution with which you have been involved—grade school, high school, college, professional school, church, synagogue, etc. You may find a use for your story as did the author of the welcoming bulletin from the Chapel by the Sea in Florida.

Welcome to the
Captiva Chapel by the Sea!

Nondenominational services of worship are conducted here from the third Sunday in November to the third Sunday in April, at 11 a.m. The pulpit is filled by retired clergymen of various denominations, who are in residence for the season.

HISTORY

This building, under the palms and gumbo limbos along the Gulf of Mexico, was originally a county school, then a Methodist mission. It was reorganized in 1948 by a local group, purchased in 1954, and continues to be managed by an incorporated Board of 15 Associates, elected for 3 year terms. In several steps the building was repaired, enlarged, redecorated, and the parsonage with pastor's study and garage added. The adjoining cemetery was improved.

There is no membership roster. Support is provided entirely by plate collections and other voluntary gifts.

One of the treasured traditions of the Chapel is a Christmas Eve service, concluding with a procession with lighted candles to gather about an illuminated tree in the Chapel yard for carol singing.

2. Write a history of your town, county, or some area with which you are familiar. You will undoubtedly need to do additional research, just as you did for family history. (The techniques from that chapter will apply.) For instance, W. B. Bowden, a long-time resident of Bainbridge Island in Washington, published his history of Port Madison, a community founded there in 1854. He included details of the New England lumbermen who came around the Horn to become the first white settlers, of the Indian tribe they found there and made their friends, of the growth and then the decline of the lumber business in the area, and so on. He illustrated the booklet with old photographs, sketches and early maps.

3. Choose some subjects for history from among the dozen here, or add others of your own—

- an antique, a painting, some interesting artifact
- a game (Scrabble, a child's game, one newly popular)
- a national park, a famous garden
- a resort, an old restaurant, a favorite haunt
- an old building, a National Historic Site
- a club, business, some organization
- a community tradition (Sytende Mai in a Norwegian town, an ethnic holiday in your town)
- a battalion, regiment, ship in the Civil War, World War I or II
- a car—one you owned, or the history of an old model or obsolete car such as the Edsel ("My father's first car was called a Mason-Maytag. Whether it was related to the washing machine . . . ")
- a museum (local, state, national, private)
- a breakthrough, a discovery in science, medicine, botany, etc. (a new archaeological dig, development of hybrid corn, etc.)

You're on your own! Free to find a world of new subjects for exploration through research, free to roam the past in imagination, free to introduce your interests and discoveries to readers near and far.

Chapter 10

Writing Poetry

*I*n 1888 Walt Whitman wrote, "No one will get at my verses who insists upon viewing them as a literary performance." That's a modest statement from the man who begins one of his works with "I celebrate myself, and sing myself." Yet his comment is a good starting point for a section on writing poetry.

Most of us think of ourselves as "meat and potatoes" writers. We write acceptable, commonsensical prose—warm and nourishing. But we feel unequal to what we think of as the imaginative, gourmet specialties of poetry.

Just what is poetry anyway? Lynn Z. Bloom ponders this in "Definition of Poetry," and, like many of us, finds it undefinable.

Definition of Poetry

Once
I took a course in aesthetics
Three hours credit
If I could learn
What a poem was.

A poem was "the record of the best and happiest
  moments of the best and happiest minds";

"The best words in the best order";
"A criticism of life."
But what was "best"?
Would "happiness" necessarily dwell in a criticism?
And if a poem "tells us . . . something that cannot
    be said," how could we discuss the ineffable?

A poem was a poem, we learned, if it made you feel
    as if the top of your head were taken off,
Or if your spine tingled
Or your gut quivered,
Save the classics, and with them, the more
    cathartic, the better.

A poem was metered, rhythmic, regular—
Except free verse.
A poem rhymed—
But not blank verse.
A poem had consonance, assonance, alliteration,
    onomatopoeia—
Or none of these.

A poem used a "higher concentration of imagery"
    than prose.
"But how high is high?" asked we bourgeois
    gentlemen, speakers of prose all our lives.
A poem was "poem-shaped,"
Yes, just as a human being was man-shaped,
    unless she was a woman.
Finally, we were told, "a poem should not mean,
    but be."
Be what?

To answer the question for myself
I wrote a term paper.
"A Definition of Poetry."
The instructor gave it an A.

But I never wrote
A poem.

Just so—like Bloom, we may never understand exactly what makes a poem, but we can still write one. Whitman's statement, too, reminds us that every poem does not have to be a masterpiece. This is not to suggest that we rid ourselves of our love and appreciation for the great writers, but that we free ourselves from thinking we must write like them. For poetry is many things and it belongs to everyone. It ranges from the simplest songs and rhymes and ballads, with meters that make us tap our feet and swing our arms and sing, to the sweeping lines of great thought by Homer and Shakespeare. And it is many things in between. Above all, it is for everyone to enjoy and to write and to share.

What's it like to write poetry? Had Manske, former insurance executive who has published several books of poetry since his retirement, tells why and how he started.

Nature Poems . . . How Come?

Before we found the old farm, millions of words had clattered through the typewriters or were sucked away by dictaphones. Words in want ads and newspaper display, magazines and direct mail plus the flood of memos and reports required in 40 years of advertising. All of it was writing for work.

Writing for fun began with the old farm.

Every abandoned place acquires a magic of its own. The ground fog that glows ghostly against the rising sun across the meadow and the goblins that hoot like barred owls in the black night have messages of their own that need to be told.

Life on the old farm is a little like experiencing genesis and watching creation continue. It's a world of its own. With its own change and swing. Its own light and dark. As in the beginning

> *. . . early morning mists*
> *wreathe dark dew glistened rocks*

while night shapes hide
in hemlocks on the shore. Bats
that flickered in the cool owl hours
are gone and cricket clocks
drowse to a stop. Leaf end drops
make quiet rings as light turns up
behind the saw-tooth tamaracks.

Nature, of course, abhors a void. When cultivation stops, wildness quickly creeps back. Sooner or later man loses the battle and learns that he is expendable. As has been said, nature does not need him but goes on at its primal pace, sauntering to its own music like

. . . spring rain violins
the hyla chorus shrill in deepened dusk,
and distance-gentled mating drum in May
that's almost like a throb in the inner ear.

Overall, the old farm abides in contentment. Despite the bickering among the blue jays, it is a quiet, peaceful place. Urban noise and urgency is absent. Rhythm is all, a common thing.

It's pulse, like hearts
that throb iambically
and suns that daily arc
to make way for the moon.

Tides flow, retreat, as if
the earth slowly inhales
then lets its breath. Fall
waltzes winter around the year;
lifetimes and dynasties march
up and down again. Galaxies grow
before they soften to a glow.
Like breathing in and breathing out.

And it's delightful to write about.

The Stuff of Poetry

What is the subject matter of poetry? What do poets write about? Where does a poem begin? For Had Manske, it began with the farm, and, by extension, nature—a never-ending source of subject matter for innumerable poets. But it can be anything, absolutely anything. T. S. Eliot's poems about cats, comparing those feline creatures to human beings, inspired the recent musical; Donald Hall wrote an ode which he called "O Cheese," interweaving into his lines the names of some seventeen varieties of cheeses. Like these poets, you can find the stuff of poetry in your everyday life. As you read the poems here, you will see how the poet notices something other people overlook and makes a poem of it.

Peter Meinke compares two unlikely candidates: Lord Byron, poet of the nineteenth century, and Joe DiMaggio, baseball great of the twentieth. What could they possibly have in common? The poet tells us.

Byron vs. DiMaggio

Yesterday I was told
the trouble with America is that
these kids here
would rather be DiMaggio
than Byron: this shows our decadence.

But I don't know,
there's not that much difference.
Byron also would have married Monroe
or at least been in there trying;
he too covered a lot of territory,
even with that bum foot,
and made the All-European swimming team
in the Hellespont League.

> *And, on the other hand, you*
> *have to admit that DiMag played*
> *sweet music*
> *out there in the magic grass*
> *of centerfield.*

Meinke begins with a generalization he has heard about the younger generation's choice of heroes, then disproves the point with a very few facts: Byron's athletic ability as a swimmer and his reputation as a lover set against DiMaggio's fame as a hitter and his marriage to Marilyn Monroe. The poet does this with a freshness of vocabulary, making Byron's swim a "League" event and DiMag's skill a "sweet music." The impact of this poem, like that of many others, lies in making readers aware of something they've never thought of before.

- *Try this*—Think of two or three unlikely comparisons: cook/magician; auto mechanic/surgeon; Pandora's box/computer. List some facts about each, then choose those fresh likenesses that you can use to make a point. Put your thoughts into the form of a poem.

As you have discovered with Peter Meinke's stanzas, many poems carry their meaning by implication, not by the more direct statements you are used to in prose. In six lines, high school student Marguerite Kelly made a point about her "Religion Class."

> *They told me to write about life;*
> *To discover new insights;*
> *To probe my inner soul;*
> *To meditate on my faith;*
> *To reflect on my ideals;*
> *And have it in by Friday.*

• *Try this*—Drawn from an everyday experience, this poem is a simple list of requirements for an assignment. Ask yourself how the zinger in the final line relates to the list.

List several things you have done or several you are expected to do. Put the items on your list in parallel structure as Kelly does (she introduces each point with *to*). Notice how parallelism gives the lines a balance and rhythm. Use some or all of the items from your list and "add them up" for a final surprise comment.

Edgar Lee Masters' *Spoon River Anthology* is a series of biographical sketches in the form of "dramatic monologue," allowing the characters to speak for themselves as "I." Meet one of them.

Lucinda Matlock

I went to the dances at Chandlerville,
And played snap-out at Winchester.
One time we changed partners
Driving home in the moonlight of middle June
And then I found Davis.
We were married and lived together for
      seventy years,
Enjoying, working, raising the twelve children,
Eight of whom we lost
Ere I had reached the age of sixty.
I spun, I wove, I kept the house, I nursed the sick,
I made the garden, and for holiday
Rambled over the fields where sang the larks,
And by Spoon River gathering many a shell,
And many a flower and medicinal weed—
Shouting to the wooded hills, singing to the
      green valleys.

> At ninety-six I had lived enough, that is all,
> And passed to a sweet repose.
> What is this I hear of sorrow and weariness,
> Anger, discontent and drooping hopes?
> Degenerate sons and daughters,
> Life is too strong for you—
> It takes life to love Life.

- *Try this*—Count, at least roughly, the number of details packed into the twenty-two lines of the poem. What impressions of Lucinda Matlock do you get from the details? Think of a few adjectives that precisely sum up those impressions.

  Choose a person, real or imagined, and tell that person's story in a monologue. Use details (you may need to list some first, then choose among them) that reveal what that person was or is like. Be brief; pack it in as Masters does.

  Notice that Lucinda Matlock's ideas about life are presented as a direct statement in the last line. If you can, use the details of your poem to lead to a dramatic conclusion.

  An option: make your "I" yourself; tell your story in a "memoir poem."

Masters' poem builds with details, phrased in more or less parallel fashion. These accumulate to lead to the final admonition. The next poem looks quite different on the page. Emma Thornton starts with a question and then gives her answer—a recipe. What could be more everyday as a subject? But see how she moves you beyond the realm of baking! Again, notice the relationship between details and idea.

Sand Tarts
You ask how I make sand tarts?
Well, I'll tell you:
    It takes one cup of butter,
    two cups of sugar,
    three cups of flour,
    four eggs—save one white;
And:
    it takes well-refrigerated dough,
    cool tools,
    a lightly-floured board—
And:
    at least a year's supply of patience,
    understanding of the value of tradition,
    and respect for my mother's hands.

- *Try this*—Just as the recipe, and the work of following it, brings something good to the table, so a poem usually offers you something poignant, perhaps powerful, something to think about, even to treasure. Recipes, of course, might not be about food. This one was written by Sadie Carlson as the frontispiece of a church cookbook.

Recipe for Daily Living
Each morning
Take a generous portion
Of the bread of Life
From Chapter 6 of St. John's Gospel.
At noon
Take a drink
From the fountain of living water
Found in the Book of Revelation 7:17.
In the evening
Add seasonings from Colossians 4:6.
The result will be strength
To meet the problems of life.

Both recipe poems carry messages, although not all poems do so as directly as these. Perhaps you, as many others, like such messages, even expect them. Write a recipe-poem to carry a bit of your philosophy or advice. You might start by asking yourself what recipe (or prescription) you think leads to happiness, success, good marriage, living amiably with someone or some group, adjusting to the unexpected, or something similar.

Moments of heightened experience frequently prompt a poetic response, the expression of an overflow of feeling. Poets capture these feelings both for themselves and their readers as William Wordsworth did in the spring of 1804.

Daffodils

I wandered lonely as a cloud
That floats on high o'er vales and hills,
When all at once I saw a crowd,
A host, of golden daffodils;
Beside the lake, beneath the trees,
Fluttering and dancing in the breeze.

Continuous as the stars that shine
And twinkle on the milky way,
They stretched in never-ending line
Along the margin of a bay:
Ten thousand saw I at a glance,
Tossing their heads in sprightly dance.

The waves beside them danced; but they
Out-did the sparkling waves in glee:
A poet could not but be gay,
In such a jocund company:
I gazed—and gazed—but little thought
What wealth the show to me had brought:

For oft, when on my couch I lie
In vacant or in pensive mood,

They flash upon that inward eye
Which is the bliss of solitude;
And then my heart with pleasure fills,
And dances with the daffodils.

When we read "Daffodils," we enter Wordsworth's world, seeing the flowers as he did, feeling his rapture, and carrying it away for remembrance later:

And then my heart with pleasure fills,
And dances with the daffodils.

We respond to many of the same things—beauty, especially in nature; and the universal feelings of love and loss. Wordsworth felt a joy in nature; Murilla Weronke expresses loneliness over her granddaughter's departure.

On Leah Leaving at Age Seven
I found the blossom where you
     dropped it.
It lay on the walk where you said,
"They're lovely. I never really looked at
     them before."
I cried a little for it and me
     because we both looked so lonely.
But then I thought—what good to cry?
     summertime flowers will come again—
And so, my sweet, will you.

Notice how Murilla embodies the experience, showing what happened that led to her feelings rather than talking about them. In this way she helps us see what happened and understand why she felt as she did, without saying sentimentally, "Poor me." Here again, as in all your writing, it is better to show than to tell. Or think of it another way: the telling comes implicitly with effective showing.

- *Try this*—Think back, perhaps to your journal and memoirs and moments you recorded there. Or think of experiences and times you have written about. Choose an occasion of deep feeling to describe in a poem.

Special occasions give rise to poems in another way. Just as England's poet laureate writes poems for such events as a coronation or the queen's birthday, you in a more modest way may like to write for special days in your life, or in the life of others. Jessie Farnham wrote this tribute to Robert Frost for such a special day.

For an Eighty-Seventh Birthday

What beauty the world would have lost
If God had omitted Robert Frost!
God must have thought when He willed his birth:
"I shall send a singer to soothe the earth;
I shall send a toiler whose work will yield
Rich, warm soil for a brighter field;
He will be a poet whose voice will ring
As though refreshed by Pierian spring;
And his words will linger long past the day
Their vibrant echoes have died away."
And He must have known that the man would be
Shoulder-deep in simplicity,
With head in the clouds and feet on a rock
And a heart that ticks with Eternity's clock.

- *Try this*—Write an occasional poem in anticipation of an event or to commemorate one: birth, birthday, anniversary, retirement, graduation, friendship, and so on. By writing such poems you can create greeting cards more personal than commercial ones. In your poems, show why the person is special; include references to actual events; be warm and sincere. Of course, you'll want to consider these same qualities if you're writing for a public occasion as you would for a personal one: a reunion, the presentation of an award, the dedication of a building or park, and so on.

If it is suitable, try humor in your occasional poem as the writer of this limerick did for a teacher-friend who was retiring.

> *There once was a lady named Char*
> *Whose talents were known wide and far,*
>   *Her ways providential*
>   *Brought results exponential:*
> *No students now write below par.*

The Form of Poetry

In defining poetry, Lynn Bloom explains that a "poem is 'poem-shaped.' " In the poems so far you have observed several poetic forms, but most of them are what we call "free verse." Although free verse can have many metrical and musical devices, it does not follow a prescribed form. The poet is free to suit the pattern to the content. This is probably what you have been doing in the preceding activities.

The **limerick**, one of those familiar forms, is a favorite for humorous verse. The pattern is fixed: five lines, with the first, second and fifth rhyming; and the third and fourth, which are shorter, rhyming. The accented syllables, too, are spaced according to rule. Limerick writers often take liberty with the language, changing words or creating new ones. The form is meant to be fun, as this anonymous writer in one of our workshops knew:

> *There was a young lady named Lane*
> *Went to doctors with many a pain*
> *Their only suggestion—*
> *"Ignore your digestion,*
> *And take a fall trip out to Maine."*

Another form that you may play with is the **haiku**. A very old Japanese form dating back to the thirteenth century, haiku is a poem of three lines with 5-7-5 syllables respectively, for a total of seventeen. The poem carries a single image, often drawn from nature and creating a single impression or mood. These examples are from Beth, a member of one of our workshops:

The Valentine

Lace encircled hearts
capture antique sentiments
framed on blue velvet.

Wisteria

Fading purple petals fall
profusely decorating
the patio floor.

Like artists who find their models unexpectedly in the common (Andy Warhol's painting of a can of soup), poets sometimes play with prose passages to create what we call **found poems**. Specifically, the poet selects a promising passage, lifts it from its natural habitat, and copies it into whatever poetic form seems effective. It is permissible to repeat, delete, and rearrange, but not to add anything. This "found poem" was derived from a sign tacked on several neighborhood posts and trees:

Our Milo

Lost—loved—lost
Family pet Milo.

Black cocker
Curly coat
Tags
On red collar.

Reward—
Generous reward!
Call—call—call
Our loved Milo!

Poets sometimes put their words into **poem shapes** to suggest the pattern of the subject they are writing about—an ice cream cone, an airplane, a pyramid. You may identify with Benjamin Hochman's experience in "Footwork."

Footwork

I can
descend
these steps
but one
by one.
There was
a time
I'd fly
down two
by two.
Does this
mean that
my race
is near-
ly run?
And what
I owe
the pi-
per now
is due?
Yet, when
at last,
I reach
the bot-
tom stair,
and see outside a pretty face or thigh,
I bid farewell to thoughts of dark despair,
and dash off as I did in days gone by.

Ballads, the story-poems you often hear in song, have a long history. Their traditions date back to folk stories passed along by word of mouth for many generations. Today you know them in the ballads of Burl Ives, the frontier songs of Pete Seeger, the cowboy songs of Carl Sandburg, the medieval ballads and modern ones sung by Joan Baez. This poem by Thomas Hardy follows some of the ballad traditions to make an ironic comment on war.

The Man He Killed

"Had he and I but met
By some old ancient inn,
We should have sat us down to wet
Right many a nipperkin!

"But ranged as infantry,
And staring face to face,
I shot at him as he at me,
And killed him in his place.

"I shot him dead because—
Because he was my foe,
Just so; my foe of course he was;
That's clear enough; although

"He thought he'd 'list, perhaps,
Off-hand like—just as I—
Was out of work—had sold his traps—
No other reason why.

"Yes, quaint and curious war is!
You shoot a fellow down
You'd treat if met where any bar is,
Or help to half-a-crown."

Ballads are metrical and rhymed. The usual form stipulates a four-line stanza with the second and fourth rhymed, four strong accents in lines one and three, three accents in lines two and four. Hardy varies this, as do many ballad writers, to rhyme both first and third, second and fourth lines. Many ballads are in dialogue; many use first person as storyteller, as Hardy does. The form is fun to play with and invites singing and reading aloud.

- *Try this*—Experiment with one or more of these forms to carry thoughts, pictures or stories of your own. Don't allow your poem to be enslaved by the form. Your thought or image is still uppermost.

  Special for a writing group: Select a piece of prose for everyone to use as the basis of a found poem. Share your poems (the different versions) in the group.

  Special for ballad lovers: Read and listen to ballads, look further into ballad forms and traditions. Choose a regional or family story to put into a ballad of your own.

Precepts for Poets

The Enjoyment

- Reading and listening to poetry, and loving it, prepares you for writing. Look at poems on the page; listen to recordings; go to readings, take time to respond.
- Being a good observer—cultivating the senses and imagination—is a valuable attribute. Use your antennae. Keep open to experience.

The Content

- Anything in the world can be the subject of poetry. By means of imagination and feeling the poet discovers a wide range of content.
- Most poems focus—limit content to single experiences, to a distillation of thought or emotion.
- Poetry uses facts, but it doesn't stop there. Its purpose is more than simply to inform.
- The poet's feeling about the poem and its content is essential to an effective poem. The feeling guides the poet, infuses the poem.

The Words

- "The best words in the best order"—this is the phrase Samuel Taylor Coleridge used to describe the language of poetry.
- Every word counts in poetry, where ideas are compressed into small spaces.
- The poet chooses words for precision, imagery, vividness, power; but this does not mean that the language should be artificial or overly-elegant.
- Poems often start in discovering likeness, in metaphor, and they use language to convey this surprise to the reader.
- Poets use words for their sound as well as meaning. They create word music through such devices as rhyme, meter, alliteration, repetition, and refrain.

The Forms

- Poetic forms are solid or fluid, prescribed or free. Knowing the traditional forms—or the traditions in forms—is of value to the poet, who is free to use them or to move out to experiment or invent.
- The shape the poem assumes should be related to the content and to the effect the poet wants to produce on and in the reader.
- Rhyme and meter are tools of poetry to be used properly, not artificially. The tools should not control—they should serve the meaning and purpose.

The Effects

- Poems may start in inspiration—in sudden response—and they may be short. But their power and effect are invariably the result of working and reworking. First vision is enhanced through revision.
- A finished poem carries with it a sense of rightness to the eye and ear as well as to the mind and heart.

Chapter 11

Writing Stories

$\mathcal{E}$veryone likes hearing or reading good stories. Probably you like to tell them as well. You may like them long or short, fantastic or mysterious or realistic. Stories extend imagination, provide an escape, or lead to new acquaintances and new worlds, for they have a life of their own. And in writing a story you can create a world, put the characters in it, direct their actions and reactions as you determine what happens. You are the puppeteer and you pull the strings.

Flannery O'Connor, noted short story writer, has said that in any discussion of the short story we must consider what we mean by short. She warns that even if a story is short, it should not be slight. A good story leaves something important in the reader's mind—an impression, an experience, or a meaning.

It is detail that gives the reader the experience of a story, and capturing that detail—showing rather than telling—is perhaps the most necessary part of story telling. You can find details in your own life, in the lives of others, in all you observe around you. Use them to create a new world—that of the story.

The impulse to tell a story may come from anything or many things—from an event with a twist, or one lost and then remembered; or one you wonder about and want to follow up in imagination; from observing someone who would make a good character; from a thought, perhaps a quotation that to you is particularly meaningful; from something as small as an ad for a lost dog, or a letter in an advice column. No one needs to give you ideas; they are all around you. We can't give you the impulse. We can encourage you not to ignore that impulse.

Nor can we give you a formula for a successful story, a recipe or rule to guide what you write or how. You can begin, though, by considering the elements of a story and by reading good examples.

The Elements of a Story

In school you probably talked about story elements and defined them like this:

> Characters—or character (for you may have only one), the imagined people who walk your pages
>
> Plot—the arranged events, the action or conflict that must be resolved
>
> Setting—the backdrop, the locale of the story, the environment for the characters
>
> Theme—what the story adds up to; the idea behind the story and growing out of it. This doesn't have to be stated; it should be sensed or felt.
>
> Point of view—the vantage point from which the author tells the story. We speak of these as omniscient—seeing all; limited omniscient—narrowing the view, usually to one character (these are told in third person); first person narrator—seeing only what the "I" who tells the story can know.

A Story

"Perpetual Care" is by Hazel F. Briggs , an "elderwriter" who has written on and off all her life. Modestly, she says that she "has had only intermittent publication." This story first appeared in *The Wisconsin Academy Review*, and it was later reprinted in Mrs. Briggs' collection of stories, *I'll Tell You Tomorrow.*

Perpetual Care

The Slocum plot in Welton (pop. 3827) was unquestionably impressive. Whenever she visited the cemetery, Mrs. Slocum was pleased with its prominent location on a slight mound near the main entrance where several paths and roads converged. Whether chosen purposely or otherwise, it was apparent that visitors to the cemetery had to pass the plot on their way to other destinations.

In the center was a tall, spired monument with the name SLOCUM prominently engraved upon it, under which were the birth and death dates of Amos and Abby Slocum, her parents-in-law, who had founded the family. Grouped around this central stone were a number of identical modest headstones under which lay the sons, their wives, a daughter, her husband, and other progeny of the third and even fourth generation who had been gathered to the Lord.

This concentration of the family always gave Mrs. Slocum a feeling of strength and importance. As the years went by and she was finally the only living member of the older generation, her sense of closeness to the family plot increased. Each time she visited the cemetery and saw her own headstone already in place with only the date of death missing, Libby Slocum felt comforted in the knowledge that, regardless of earthly calamity, an eternal resting place was ready and waiting for her.

No matter how often she visited the cemetery, she never failed to applaud the foresight which Amos Slocum had shown in buying this beautiful location. She remembered him as a man who liked to have his affairs tied up neatly. In spite of a tremendous zest for life, Amos had had a respectful regard for the decorum of death. And so he had bought "perpetual care" for the plot when he acquired it for himself and his family at the turn of the century. At that time, Libby Slocum had been a young and very uncertain bride. She had married Albert only for security, and the luxury inherent in "perpetual care" had grown to be a lasting comfort.

As she stood at her husband's grave, however, shortly after his death, perpetual care for the first time did not seem adequate. Perpetual care was a leveling factor for high and low alike regardless of merit or quality, and to Mrs. Slocum such equality now seemed wholly unsatisfactory. Although she had never cared for any of the Slocums, including her husband Albert, Libby had never felt that they were of equal merit, and she resented the total absence of evaluation as exemplified in the identical headstones and perpetual care.

During Amos' lifetime the difference in the ages of the brothers had been a distinguishing factor. Amos had been the head of the family. It was he who had acquired the substantial family fortune. In fact, he had represented the entire Slocum family. But after Amos "passed away" in 1909 at the age of eighty-seven, some competitive interest had developed among his sons, although no feeling of superiority—if any existed—had ever been shown.

Each brother, as well as his one daughter, had received an equal share of Amos' worldly goods and during the ensuing year there had been no more than quiet speculation regarding the extent to which each had increased or decreased his substance. Was Thomas, the banker, more prosperous than landowner Edward? Or Albert, the farmer, worth more than Henry, the implement dealer?

Albert and Libby had often discussed these matters and had, in fact, frequently fretted under their inability to arrive at a correct answer. But no answer to these questions was forthcoming during the lifetime of any of the brothers, since each member of the family kept his affairs strictly to himself. Frugal living had always been the Slocum way of life, and this ingrained habit had successfully concealed any change that might have occurred in anyone's financial status. But as death claimed one after the other, carefully guarded secrets had been revealed, and the surviving brothers and sister had learned, at least to some extent, how much the departed had acquired by the size of the estate bequeathed to his heirs.

Now Libby Slocum had all these facts at her disposal. She remembered the exact evaluation of each estate, including also that of Florence, Albert's only sister.

There had been times, years ago, when Libby found it galling to live by the axiom—a penny saved is a penny earned—but such emotions were too distant to recall. Libby had long since become a real Slocum. As such, she felt when she visited the cemetery where each brother lay inconspicuously under his headstone, that some recognition should be given to individual performance.

Another reason also motivated her. Since Albert's death and her acquisition of his substantial fortune, her affection for him had considerably increased, and she felt an urgent need to show him honor. If he had been the least successful of Amos' sons, it might have been otherwise. As it was, she knew that Albert would rate well in comparison with his brothers. Hence some outward display on her part would be a fitting gesture of gratitude to him for her own present well-being and freedom. In spite of a family reticence which had restrained Albert, at times almost to the point of inaction, she believed he would now appreciate recognition, especially if she employed the family's own scale of values—how much money each of the brothers had left when he died.

But the actual medium to be employed evaded her. Mrs. Slocum did not intend to be ostentatious. Since in Albert's lifetime she had never spent a cent except under his critical supervision, extravagance would be conscienceless. In fact, extravagance was hard to learn at seventy-five.

Twice she engaged Charlie Biddle, who rented one of her farms, to drive her to the cemetery where she could study the problem. On the second visit she approached the subject obliquely.

"It looks kind of monotonous, don't you think?" she asked, waving her black cotton-gloved hand over the identical headstones.

"I dunno," said Biddle. "It looks pretty good. The grass is nice and green." He scratched his head thoughtfully. "It looks real good."

"That's the perpetual care," explained Mrs. Slocum. "The cemetery's got to do that. They've been paid to cut the grass and trim round the stones forever."

"Oh," said Biddle. He was well aware that if the Slocums had paid for something they would get their money's worth.

"What I mean is," continued Mrs. Slocum, "there don't seem to be enough difference between them."

"Their names're all there," answered the farmer, scanning the headstones. "You can't get them mixed up. You can even figure out how old they was, if you want to."

Mrs. Slocum did not pursue the subject. She felt it would not be fitting.

During the following winter, however, she thought about her problem a great deal without success. But when spring came and the country-side began to bud and flower, a logical solution presented itself—one which she knew would meet with Albert's wholehearted approval because it was simple, cheap, and extremely fair.

From the local florist she bought six flower pots, varying in price from a dollar seventy-five for a very large one, to fifty cents for a relatively small one. She had each pot filled with a red geranium plant, varying also in size according to the size of the flower pot. Over the graves of each of the Slocums (spouses were excluded) she decided to place a pot of flowers, strictly and honestly according to the deceased's importance.

Only Amos would get a dollar seventy-five pot with a large plant in it. Albert and Edward, equally successful, would each get a dollar-and-quarter pot. Henry, who had died well off but not as wealthy, would get an eighty-five-cent pot, while Thomas and Florence would get fifty-cent pots respectively. Thomas had died bankrupt during the 1933 depression and therefore surely merited only a small pot. Yet, this decision bothered Mrs. Slocum a little. She remembered that after Thomas' death, some land which Albert had previously accepted from him in lieu of a ten-thousand-dollar defaulted note, had later yielded a handsome profit. However, facts were facts. Thomas had not had a penny to his name when he died. Mrs. Slocum salved her conscience by putting an extra nice plant into the small container. As for Florence, she had never distinguished herself by marriage or otherwise. A fifty-cent pot went to her merely because she had been a Slocum.

All told, the transaction cost six dollars and ten cents for the flower pots and five-fifty for plants. She then paid Biddle a dollar to drive her to the cemetery on Memorial Day to help arrange the offerings. After each pot had been placed squarely and conspicuously on its designated grave, Mrs. Slocum was sure that anyone would recognize the relative importance of each member of the family. It was a good job well worth the price.

On July Fourth she paid the farmer fifty cents, because there would be no pots to carry, to take her to the cemetery. A first glance revealed that all was not well. Not only were some of the plants in poor shape, but even worse, the pots had been moved. The big one, so carefully stationed over Amos' grave, now stood on the wrong side of the monument. Albert's plant had practically died except for a few feeble leaves as it leaned against Libby's headstone . Edward's rested on an unassigned bit of land. Only Thomas' geranium was blooming beautifully just where it had been put.

"Oh, dear," she said in her sharp, thin voice. "Look what they've done."

"Some of them don't look so good," commented

Biddle. *"It's been too dry."*

Mrs. Slocum did not answer. She took off her gloves without a word and started moving the pots around. The farmer watched her tug at the largest pot for a moment. Then he lifted it up and put it back on Amos' grave.

When all were again in place and Mrs. Slocum had watered the plants from a nearby spigot, she opened her purse and gave Biddle a half dollar.

"It wasn't that much work," protested Biddle. "You don't need to pay."

"Keep it," she answered. "I don't like to be beholden. Besides," she added thoughtfully, "we'll have to arrange about taking the pots in around Labor Day or they'll crack over the winter."

The farmer put the half dollar into his pocket.

"If that's all—" he hesitated—"I have to go down to the south pasture before milking."

"That's all," said Mrs. Slocum.

For the next five years Mrs. Slocum and whoever rented the farm made intermittent pilgrimages to the cemetery, tugging and lugging pots back to their rightful places. She complained occasionally at the cemetery office that they had been moved contrary to her wishes, but complaints yielded no results.

In a small black book in which she kept her accounts, the figures on "Flowers for Cemetery" steadily mounted. When she calculated the total sum spent, it came to well over seventy dollars!

In the middle of August, shortly after her eightieth birthday, the Fosters, her next door neighbors and dearest friends, invited Mrs. Slocum to ride with them to the cemetery. They dropped her off at the Slocum plot to return later and pick her up. She saw at once that Amos' dollar-seventy-five-cent pot

*stood in full bloom on the grave of Walter Cleggett,
Florence's insignificant husband.*

*This final insult brought tears of rage to Mrs.
Slocum's eyes. She seated herself slowly on one of
the headstones. Never before had responsibility so
oppressed her, and for a moment she was tempted
to abandon the whole thing. But—the pots had
been paid for and, more important, they had
become for her a significant symbol.*

*The August sun beat down on her black straw
hat and nearly made her sick. The glare on the
white stone monument sent shimmering figures
weaving before her eyes. She looked at the miscre-
ant flower pot and hated it. But she knew that duty
could not be denied.*

*After a few moments she tucked a strand of
white hair tightly behind one ear, laid her purse and
gloves beside the headstone where she sat and got
to her feet. She walked over to the flower pot that
stood on Walter Cleggett's grave, stooped over,
and gave it a slight turn to ease it from the ground. It
was not a pot she had lifted before—and it was
heavy, very heavy. But she managed to get hold of it
and take it into her arms. Once upright, she could
hardly see above the foliage and flowers that
brushed against her face with their pungent odor.
Staggering under the weight of her burden, she
moved towards the monument.*

*As she crossed the level ground where her own
headstone stood, a projecting tree root caught her
foot and she fell. The pot crashed to the ground.
Mrs. Slocum's head hit sharply against the
headstone.*

*On Memorial Day of the following year the Fos-
ters put a large pot of red geraniums on Mrs. Slocum's grave.*

A Closer Look

The impulse—the start of the story. Most of us know a Mrs. Slocum—the person who constantly carries an air of "I am better than thou." It may seem that knowing someone like her was the impulse for Mrs. Briggs' humorous and human story. But when we asked, "Did you start with the character as many writers do?" she smiled and said no—she got to thinking about the futility of the words "perpetual care." So here plot and characters were imagined in response to a thought, a theme. But no element works singly.

Plot—plots are said to have a rising action and falling action, an intensifying of a conflict and then a resolution of it. The plot carries us forward through a series of events, building suspense that unwinds as the story ends. Notice that each time Mrs. Slocum attempts to show her family's superiority, something frustrates her. The final frustration leads to our realization—if not hers!—of an old, old truth: all persons are eventually "leveled." How, then, does that old truth come out of the plot—the narrative line or action of the story? Would you call that the theme of the story?

Viewpoint—Mrs. Briggs tells this story from "outside"—that is, she writes in third person. But she does so chiefly through Mrs. Slocum, the central character—getting inside her thoughts, and showing the actions of others only in relationship to her. What, for instance, do you know about Mr. Biddle? How do you know what he thinks? How would it differ if told in first person by Mrs. Slocum, or Mr. Biddle, or the Fosters?

The setting—the scene of a story is more than just place. It is the environment in which characters act out their conflicts. In this story it is not only location, but atmosphere. Authors seldom describe the setting all at once. Rather, they let the reader see it gradually as the story progresses. You'll notice that the first sentence of Mrs. Briggs' story gives an exact location, but with the second sentence Mrs. Slocum and her visits to this setting become the focus of attention. Check to see how many times the setting is reintroduced with additional details to let you get the picture. Could you draw the cemetery? Locate the stones? How significant is setting to the action and to the overall effect of the story?

Characters—the characters "people" the pages of stories, but they are not people. In a realistic story like Hazel Briggs', characters may seem real. Sometimes authors who have models in mind feel they must make disclaimers—saying "any resemblance to persons living or dead is purely coincidental." But behind real-seeming characters (not the stereotypes of good guy/bad guy in fairy stories and far-fetched tales or movies) is the writer's observation and understanding of how people act in life situations.

In "Perpetual Care" you can find all the essential ways an author has of making characters come to life for a reader:

- author's comments—recall Mrs. Briggs' sentence: "In fact, extravagance was hard to learn at seventy-five."

- author's description—"Libby Slocum had been a young and uncertain bride."

- character's thoughts—"Libby Slocum felt comforted" and "She knew that Albert would rate well in comparison."

- character's action—"She bought six flower pots, varying in price."

- character's speech—"There don't seem to be enough difference" and "I don't like to be beholden."

- comments of other characters—"Their names're all there . . . You can't get them mixed up." (Mr. Biddle).

- thoughts of other characters—"He was well aware that if the Slocums had paid for something they would get their money's worth."

By taking a close look, you can see how Mrs. Briggs interweaves all the elements to achieve the impact she desired. Once the story is set in motion, once the character of Mrs. Slocum is introduced, the ending follows almost inevitably. The irony that hits us in the last two paragraphs brings surprise, but leaves a sense of rightness.

Try Your Hand at Writing a Story

Warming up—

Think about the techniques Mrs. Briggs uses and try some of them in brief writing of your own:

- play with retelling part of "Perpetual Care" in another person: Mrs. Slocum or Mr. Biddle as "I," or through the Fosters (use third person) in a conversation remembering Mrs. Slocum.
- construct a plot diagram of "Perpetual Care" to show relationships between cause/effect—Mrs. Slocum's motives lead to what action and have what consequences?
- analyze the dialogue. What makes it realistic? Write some dialogue you might use—a snatch of conversation overheard, etc.

Exploring for ideas—

Observe, reminisce, jot down thoughts—anything that might make good story material.

- people who have fascinated you—the gifted, eccentric, colorful; those who in their situations have been determined, heroic, trapped, arrogant, guilt-ridden, etc. Find the impulses for stories in life models for characters.

- collect some quotations that might become themes—
  "The grass is always greener" to suggest a family that
  moved so frequently until the mother finally was driven
  to say "NO." "Things are in the saddle and ride man-
  kind," an idea from Emerson that suggests a story
  about excessive materialism. Some quotations suggest
  good titles.

- think of situations—funny, serious, ironic, etc.—that
  suggest conflict: a stranger comes to a small town, a
  catastrophe prompts heroism, a misdeed leads to hilar-
  ious consequences, an error in judgment causes a
  quarrel between friends. Then bring in specifics, illustrations of the situation. You will recall such conflicts or
  crises in your experience. You can also find them by
  observing and listening—a funny conversation you
  hear on the bus, a garbled message left on the answering machine, a dog fight the owners interrupt.

- tap places you know or like for possible scenes—a
  deserted house with all blinds drawn; a row of dilapi-
  dated tenements all belonging to the same landlord, a
  park with a spot for solitude, a laundromat where a
  variety of people (characters) gather at the soap
  machine. Draw a map or plan and consider situations
  that might give rise to actions there.

Writing Your Story

—Let your story linger in your mind; think of its possibilities, imagine the characters, setting and actions. Let the story
germinate before you actually start to write.

—Start wherever you wish, wherever you can. Don't
expect to write your story all at once. Jot down a bit of
conversation, make a sketch of one or more of the characters,
map the setting, outline the plot by diagram or list:

John leaves ────➤
    Mary turns to Mel for help ────➤
        Mel calls John ────➤

—Tell the story simply at first, proceeding as things come to mind. "Image" is related to imagination. Visualize setting, characters, and action. "Listen" by reading aloud as you play with dialogue.

—Leave no holes in the action. Show how each event or deed comes about so that your reader can follow the plot. Someone has said, "The simplest narrative of everyday life has all the elements of story if those events are clearly chronicled."

—Keep in mind the issues involved in the action; be sure you carry these from your mind to your readers.

—Add or insert as you need, writing some possible bits separately and then fitting them in to explain characters, reveal motives, and flesh out a picture wherever needed. There is no knowing how many such additions may be necessary.

—Work on the story until all elements of human interest, suspenseful incident, and characters' personalities and motives are smoothly revealed and united into a singleness of effect. Keep the story in focus. There is no room in the short story for side issues, sub-plots, extraneous characters. Avoid waste words, irrelevant information, excessive description. On the other hand, do not settle for too little. Action and characters should be clear.

—Give special attention to the beginning, the ending, and the title. Even though you may have them in mind from the start, you may at several points want to reconsider them.

- The beginning sentences should be striking, provocative. A first sentence (or paragraph) may introduce a character, start the action and suggest conflict, invite the reader into the scene—anything so long as it makes a reader want to read on.

- Endings, no matter how ironic or impossible, must seem plausible. All that happens in the story must add up at the end. Just as the beginning invites, the ending satisfies. The final test of focus lies in that acceptance. Endings may (and often do) surprise, but even surprise must seem inevitable. (You may have the ending in mind from the first.) Sometimes a writer tells the story in flashback: all that happens leads up to the idea or result that has been revealed in the first paragraph. Then the element of suspense comes with seeing how the action leads to that end. But no matter how you begin and end, the two enclose the story, surround all that goes between.

- The title is a matter of what you want it to do. Titles may invite, reveal, or even mystify. They may provide a humorous or philosophical twist, stretching ideas even beyond the story itself. They may state the theme of the story as Hazel Briggs does with "Perpetual Care." You can have fun with titles; you can enlighten or puzzle the reader. You can change it a dozen or more times, still be dissatisfied; or you can have it in mind from the first and never think of your story under any other masthead.

Child or adult, all of us find stories pleasurable. We love the listening and the reading as we watch action unfold, meet the characters, explore strange scenes or revisit old ones. When you have an impulse to tell a story, try it. Write it down, enjoy the telling, and you will probably find readers who will enjoy it, too.

Chapter 12

A Miscellany of Ideas

Anyone who likes to write can find opportunities and outlets for useful and pleasurable efforts. Some outlets will pay small amounts; others pay big in a sense of service and personal satisfaction. Publications where you can place your writing may be those for a general public, but many new ones specifically aimed at older adults are springing up all the time. Some of the most likely outlets are those familiar to you as a reader, as a citizen, as a member of some social, religious, or interest group.

Finding Outlets in Newspapers and Newsletters

Even though you aren't a journalist on a regular news staff, many newspapers invite features on subjects that you know something about or can research. Senior projects and trips, meetings and concerns, are increasingly popular copy, as are your various personal interests and opinions. Some newspapers use only occasional articles, but others are open for regular contribution—a column on historic spots in the region

or on early settlers, features on volunteers who make a difference, reports of upcoming activities.

Similar, of course, are the materials for a newsletter circulated to the membership of a particular organization. Here
some features may be a regular part of the layout—information
of all kinds; summaries (for instance, a report of minutes for
absentees); features on persons, projects, plans—even hopes
and gripes! Anything that needs announcing or airing will find a
home here.

Some of the most prevalent writing for older adults is that
on subjects everyone expects are of major interest: where to
live and how to live happily in retirement; how to plan and
manage financially; how to eat and exercise for continuing
health; how to meet people and cope with changes in family
and friends.

There are outlets, too, for your social and political concerns. After all, adults are vitally involved in keeping the world
safe and livable for the generations to come. Back your causes
with writing. Sound information well-presented can go a long
way toward gaining support among your readers.

A Bit of Advice:
- You're "on stage"—put your best writing forward.
- Be well-informed, clear, accurate, and as brief or long as
  is fitting.
- Keep the reader in mind—be interesting, lively, direct
  as appropriate.
- Meet your deadline if you have one; follow the guide-
  lines and practices of the outlet you write for.

Bits for Special Occasions

Some events require specialized bits of writing—your best
friend retires and you want to offer a witty toast—or roast—
at the banquet; a booklet is being compiled in honor of a

distinguished employee in your company and you want to contribute a page; you are the "introducer" for a prominent speaker at your church or town centennial, etc. And when you need one of those too-expensive special occasion cards, substitute something of your own making and your own writing. Personal greetings (poetry or prose) will usually be treasured far longer than any other.

A Bit of Advice:
- Be yourself and be sincere.
- Suit style to the occasion—be as elegant, as simple, as funny as is appropriate.
- Avoid the vague and general; use anecdotes, specific examples, colorful details.

Writing about Travel

Like the old theme on "what I did last summer," too many slides and much rambling talk may make you feel you've been to Paris or seen the Sydney opera house once too often. But good travel writing, with well-selected and organized materials, gives you information for future plans and insights into places and ways of life that you may never see. Newspapers and newsletters, again, are good outlets for travelogues, and if you keep a travel log or journal, use your personal experience in writing for others. Or help someone prepare for a trip by doing some research and pre-digesting it—provide a Baedeker for a friend, or for yourself.

A Bit of Advice:
- Don't ramble, even if you recommend a rambling walk on an exciting waterfront.
- Hit the high spots; leave something for the reader to discover.
- Size up your possible outlet; suit style and content to the purpose and publication.

Writing about Hobbies

This area is as broad as you want to make it. Here you can shine: show your expertise, lure others to adventure with you into a new field, present personalities who are your role models. Both subjects and outlets are countless. Almost every hobby has its publication or publications; and newspapers and general magazines carry features about achievements or interests. The following suggestions may get you started, but you can add to the list.

- Write about your collection, and, if possible, include pictures. Write a feature about a collector or about a shop where items are available, or do a feature on the most unusual, the hardest to find, the most valuable, or most treasured item.

- If you fish, invite another to share your favorite fishing hole. Or tell your biggest fish story. Write about equipment, give instruction in fly tying, spread the news about meetings and organizations for you and your fishing buddies. Have fun by writing a feature about "the one that got away" or about some goof or mishap you've had while fishing. Either seriously or humorously, use your mistakes to warn others.

- Extend this suggestion to almost any other sport: tennis, sailing, golf, diving, hunting, hiking, walking. Again, be clear, accurate, specific, interesting, and be sure you know when enough is enough.

- Cook up some good writing about cooking. You can find both countless topics and outlets in the "food" world: specialty cook books; men as the "new" cooks; recipes for a daughter-in-law; home-tested recipes; cooking for one, two or a tribe; the smells in grandma's kitchen; garden fresh ideas; growing and drying herbs.

- Write about
    Remodeling, restoring, well done or "remuddled"
    Woodworking, quilt making, crafts of all kinds
    Raising and training pets—dogs, cats, horses,
    unusual pets. Features about people and their pets

Writing about Reading, Listening, and Viewing

We respond to the arts—we're supposed to. And when we tell others what we think of something we've read, seen, or heard, we translate our response into recommendations. We become commentators or critics. "Do read Michener's *Alaska*. It's worth carrying all that weight around just to see how it's put together." "Go see the Muni Opera production of *The King and I*; that actor who plays the King is almost as good as Brynner."

You probably read reviews and listen to critics. Sometimes you let the critics guide you. To others you say, "No way!" You may keep a journal, or make a note in your appointment book about some things you've read or seen. You make such notes for yourself. But with a little work on your part, you will find outlets for writing you do about reading, listening, and viewing.

Writing About Reading

Although the same principles apply to reviewing in general, you probably have more occasion to write about reading than about other arts.

For Yourself

1. Get the notebook habit. Not only does a reading diary preserve thoughts and feelings about what you read, but it is a way to improve your writing.

Include some or all of these:
- dates when you read the book

- reasons for choice
- title, author, publisher, dates
- book jacket information: notes on the writer's life, other works, any explanation of the book itself
  - a note for other reading: comparisons, suggested relationships to other works. One book leads to another.

2. Write a letter to the author of something you read. Sound off, not presuming that you will send your letter.

3. List reading suggestions for the future: those books you might like to own, others you might use as gifts, those to take along.

4. If you don't keep a reading diary, at least keep a notebook of gems—quotations to use on a homemade greeting card, as a heading for a club program, on a church bulletin, to add spice to a letter, to sprinkle on the margins of a daily journal, just anywhere.

For Other Readers

Writing about reading is an easy way to reach out, to be of service.

1. Write a letter to a friend recommending a book or article you have read recently.

2. Write a review for your church bulletin on some recent acquisition in your church library, or write a review of material you want added to that library.

3. Write a review for a group of friends in a book club, suggesting a book for discussion at a meeting. Or write a book talk for that club or a similar organization.

4. Write a short article about a book you think young people would enjoy, perhaps one that teaches something entertainingly or one that helps bridge generations. Do the same about a book that you think is not worthwhile. Avoid the role and tone of censor. Rather, be a thoughtful critic even

though you have strong feelings. Maybe even try a little humor.

For instance, the title "Old Silas Marner Never Did Me Any Good" suggests one approach; "Silas Marner Isn't So Silly After All!" suggests another. These starters, too, may be apt: "I wish my grandchild would read _____." "It's time to put_____ on the shelf." "Don't sell this old classic short . . ."

5. Compile a list of readings for a certain group: a club of senior citizens, a group of prospective parents or grandparents, a society for furthering some cause. As recommender, you should become as expert as possible by browsing the articles, news reports and books on your subject.

6. Take a trip, choose a section of the country or another country and visit it through books. Compile a list (with annotations) as a reading travel guide for a friend.

7. Do a similar survey and make an annotated list for any subject that particularly interests you. Keep notes for talks as well as for your bibliography. If you give such a talk, prepare the book list as handout.

8. Join an organization attached to your library. Many groups of "Friends" are volunteers who help with library chores. Offer the group your writing services as well as your time for other tasks. Maybe they can use—

- a bibliography or reviews of available big print materials
- a newspaper feature on outreach services
- feature stories on library workers, on new automation, on activities of the "Friends" organization

9. Go public with a book review or a feature on local library services: a grant to improve services, special programs for the elderly, publicity on services to nursing homes, countless other activities.

10. For your book club, create a discussion guide on a favorite classic. Write questions for consideration, notes on author's background and historical context, summaries of comments by critics. If the group is reading the book, a quiz might be useful and fun.

A Bit of Advice

Learn from the reviews you read. This one written by Paul Chance for *Psychology Today* both gives information and lets you know why he recommends the book.

From the Trenches

Patrick Welsh teaches at T. C. Williams High School in Alexandria, Virginia. One day while beginning a lesson he heard a strange cooing sound and turned around to discover a baby sitting on the lap of one of his students. It was her baby. Welsh notes that this was not the first time a student had brought a baby to class, despite there being a rule against it. Clearly, high school is not what it once was. That is a point that Welsh makes again and again in Tales Out of School *(Viking, $15.95), a book that is bound to be compared with the John Holt classic,* How Children Fail.

Obviously the kids have changed. They hold real jobs, own and drive cars, use illegal drugs, have sex and make babies. They are more worldly, if not wiser, than in past generations; they participate in more adult activities, but they are not more adult.

But Welsh shows that it isn't just the kids who are different. Parents, too, are not what they once were. One father wanted to provide alcoholic beverages at a school function because the kids "deserve a rest." A mother called a school counselor and asked him to persuade her teenage son, who was suffering from a hangover, to get out of bed. A divorced mother who slips away with her boyfriend on weekends, leaving her two teenage daughters to fend for themselves, asked the school for help because one of the girls had taken to imitating her behavior.

The teachers may also have changed, and Welsh admits that some of them are shameful. He tells of students who included obscenities in their assigned papers. One student wrote, "This is a f--- waste of time and paper." It was a test to see if the teacher read what the students wrote. The teacher flunked.

The message of Welsh's book is that our society has changed drastically in the past 30 years, and what goes on in our schools merely reflects those changes. Our schools are different because the United States is different. It is a country in which children spend more time in front of television sets than they spend in class; in which kids come home to empty, locked houses; in which foreigners are ridiculed and racial prejudice is endemic; in which kids turn in their parents for drug abuse.

Through poignant anecdotes, Welsh shows us the American high school. More importantly, he shows us that the high school is a reflecting pool into which we may look, and see ourselves.

Writing About Other Arts

If you are an opera buff, a frequenter of galleries, a devotee of movies, you have much to write about. A few of us who remember seeing Al Jolson in *The Jazz Singer* and almost every great movie since have kept a scrapbook. And the stack of showbills in our files could be resources for a memoir or history!

You can adapt many of the suggestions for writing about reading as a start for writing about any of the arts, but here are a few additional triggers.

1. Offer to do the program notes for a concert being given by a community orchestra, chorus or church choir, soloist, etc. Do a bit of research on composers, librettists, and earlier performances.

2. Many people who once enjoyed movies find current films less than palatable. Write a guide to the season's "bests" for some group you identify as audience; or choose a single film to recommend to a friend as a "must see."

3. Our viewing is changing with the advent of the VCR, which enables us to see many reruns or films we missed. Write a review of "good rentals" or "good buys," again identifying the group for which you make recommendations. Another idea: Take a second look at a movie you saw in the past. Write about your insights—old and new—as film critic John Hartl did when he revisited *Gone with the Wind* for the twenty-sixth time.

> *I didn't miss the battle scenes this time because I was enjoying the characters too much. While my return visits to several favorite childhood epics— usually DeMille, and usually biblical—had revealed little more than artifice and tedium, "Gone with the Wind" turned out to be an unexpected delight. Of course, a lot of other people figured that out long ago.*
>
> *The truth is that everything influences what you bring to a movie: how old you are; what you've read lately; the spat you had with a friend or spouse a few hours before; whether you've got a cold; how*

*you feel about the president, foreign policy, public
schools; the theater's lack of air conditioning or
fresh popcorn.*

(Notice: wouldn't that last paragraph suggest some ways to
discuss a revisit to an old film that you might make with a friend
or two? "When I saw it the first time, I thought . . .")

4. Think back to the thrill of seeing or hearing a *first* or a
great—a play or opera, a performer or lecturer, etc.: Helen
Hayes in *Victoria Regina*, Marian Anderson in concert,
Richard Burton in *Camelot*. For yourself or another, write
about your experience. Your writing might take the form of a
revisit-review or become a short memory, a reminiscence of a
great opportunity, or whatever you want to make it.

5. Many communities present local art and crafts in small
galleries or exhibit centers. Pursue your interest in the visual
arts by volunteering as a reviewer for a local publication,
develop short explanatory notes for a display, or prepare
announcements as publicity.

6. Hollywood often takes a look at its own history, cele-
brates an anniversary—the fiftieth year for *Gone with the
Wind*, a retrospective of Bing Crosby, a birthday for George
Burns. As such occasions come along, write your own celebration or memoir for it.

Tips for Reviewing

Whether you review a book, a play, a musical performance, a movie, an art exhibit—almost anything—answering
the questions below will be appropriate. Be selective, though,
and use those that apply for your purpose. Start wherever you
wish—perhaps with a catchy quotation, a good example, your
flat-out opinion, a comment for a definite audience.

- What's it about?—summarize, but don't give every-thing away.
- What is the background or history?
- Who made it? (information about writer, composer, etc.)
- Does it have special features?
- To whom would it appeal?
- How does it compare to other productions or artifacts of the same kind?
- Into what class does it fall? (romance novel? modern jazz?)
- What is your evaluation of it—your reactions?
  From what position and attitude are you judging? Are you biased in any way? Admitting the stance you take, and supporting this by explaining the experience you have in the area, makes your argument stronger.
- What examples (excerpts, quotations, mention of high spots) support your evaluation? What examples will interest the reader of your review?

The shared writing of reviews often builds friendships as well as appreciation. As you review what you watch, read, listen to, and enjoy, you are likely to find some happy compan-ionship with other movie buffs, gallery haunters, or fellow concert goers.

One Writer's Conclusion

After tax-consultant Bob Travis retired to Florida, he continued to write occasional articles for his hometown newspaper in New York State. In reprinting this essay from the *Palmyra Courier-Journal*, we let him speak for himself—and, we hope, for you.

Why Do I Write?

As I finished his income tax forms, he asked me how I spent my time after the tax work was over in April. He was surprised that I wrote articles. Why? "I do it to satisfy my ego. I like to show off," I said.

When I said it, I realized my joking response was only partly true. I like to tell people how to do their taxes because it helps them. But the reason I write is because of my joy of living. I enjoy what I'm doing, and that is why I write.

There are advantages to being able to have something to do instead of watching TV or hanging out at poolside. Being alone for a while and having an engrossing pastime is what lots of people would pay highly for during their busy lives. It is like being able to get away from it all for a time—and it doesn't cost a thing. And, it is priceless during retirement.

We recently went to a large new apartment complex and saw the fancy club house. Their high costs and the multitude of activities don't appeal to me. If they had a lecture on economics or instruction in photography or writing, I would have been happy to go, but those ornate clubs don't dream of nutty things like that. Having a place to go to hear people talk about things that interest me would be an attraction. I'm that kind of oddball.

One of the results of my writing about the past is to awaken in me the understanding that the present is very much the same as the past. I did an income tax for a woman who wanted her live-in boarder to be entered as her dependent. She had a house in another state, a small farm, and no money to pay her taxes.

This is a modern circumstance, but not much different from what happened in my hometown in 1938. I'll never tell more than that, but my answer fifty years ago was the same I gave this lady last week—to stop coasting and drifting and start taking command of her life.

Much of my writing is an emphasis of this basic rule of mental stability founded on an honest evaluation of a person's true worth.

Another changeless factor today is that life is more rewarding as you learn to work through people and with people. Other folks are as important to an individual now as they were 50 years ago. When I read all of the books and articles that tell you how different things are today and try to make people feel sorry for themselves, I wish folks would get up at the crack of dawn and listen to sleepy birds singing the sun up. If I can get the beauty of life through to only a few folks, my efforts are well

worthwhile. *Life is still the same old quest for success and happiness. . . .*

I [often] *write about stress and how to cure it
with the basic ingredient of an honest look at one's
values and deep-seated aims for life. My reward
comes when I hear of anyone who has read about
these ideas and benefited from them. And I write to
leave an enduring heritage of my philosophy of
living. It is a good one for me, and I think it could
help others. So I try to set it down as clearly as
possible. Most of us don't get the chance to do this,
and there are thousands of people who should try it
as a lesson in what they learned from life. Even
though my writings will probably not be very enduring, the effort amuses, diverts, and busies me.*

*A constant companion of mine is the tantalizing
question, "Am I writing what others think I should
think or what I think I think? Are those my ideas
from a long life, or are they the thoughts of others
on what I should feel?" There could be a part of
both, since I am a compulsive reader and learn from
others every day I live. I also strain their ideas
through mine and come up with my own thoughts
and overtones of both.*

*Last but not least, I write to find out what I think.
All of us think in words, even though we never utter
them, and they flow steadily through our minds,
hardly showing on the surface. My problem is that I
frequently forget some of those ideas and wish I had
a record of them for reference. When I write them,
and look back on them, I have a basis for further
thoughts. My writing is an extension of a part of the
words that flow through my mind all the time.*

Appendix
Helpful Hints

"You know when you think about writing a book, you think it is overwhelming. But, actually, you break it down into tiny little tasks any moron could do." So writes Annie Dillard (the author of *Pilgrim at Tinker's Creek* and *Holy, the Firm*).

As you collect materials and work with your ideas, you, too, may be feeling overwhelmed. That's natural. How to begin? How to get organized? How to bring your work to an effective conclusion? As a reader and as a writer, you want a beginning that leads fairly logically to the ending, and within, an arrangement of parts to follow easily and naturally.

How Do I Get It All Together?

Chronological order is what you will use most often. Stories, memoirs, histories, and processes usually follow a time sequence. But surrounding that orderly progression you may use some techniques for variation.

- Devise a "framework"—a catchy beginning, perhaps a theme or anecdote that you then return to briefly at the end.

- Use a flashback—start in the present, and then go back to the beginning and trace the events in time order; you may sometimes use a back-and-forth pattern between present and past.

- Describe a process in steps—1, 2, and 3. "First you do this, and then that" is useful in explaining a hobby or giving directions.

- Choose a theme around and within which to organize your chronology.

- Collect a series of shorter chronological sections, smaller stories or events, to form the larger whole. This allows you to work in small segments and to use many stories to tell the longer one.

The chief goal, of course, is to keep time and steps both clear. Use any method or device that helps you do this:

- items on note cards to shuffle and arrange later, to recheck as you write (Color coding cards is helpful; e.g., for a memoir use blue for the events of the first years, yellow for the middle, etc.)

- an outline—more or less formal, more or less full as required

- a sketch or "road map" ("Clustering," a method of starting that you found in Chapter 7, is a "sketch" that helps you control material.)

Some writing does not follow a chronological pattern at all. Consider these other arrangements:

- List—arrange the items in order of importance (ascending or descending) or any other order you choose, including the random ("The year's best books on wellness for senior readers").

- Start with the general, follow it with supporting examples ("Many predictions from the old *Farmer's Almanacs* were right on target."—then give examples).

- Start with examples and let these lead to a conclusion. (This is reverse of the above.)

- Show the causes for some result, putting either causes or result in first position ("For several reasons, young people now delay marriage until later.").

- Group—put likes together; compare or contrast; balance likes and opposites ("Sail and motor—two stages in my life").

- Describe, picture by giving details of a scene—moving in space from detail to detail as the photographer's eye would in planning a photograph. ("Grandma was a wonder to watch. For quilt making, her hands worked flat to smooth and fit, moving perpendicular to the material to cut and sew. The yellow calico was cut with crisp care and assurance, arranged aesthetically to reveal color on display, then stitched with painstakingly small stitches to form the round that bent into another to create the double wedding ring wedded together."— from *The Store (phone 306)* by Marian Kanable and Jean Kanable Birkett.)

Select materials, discarding what doesn't fit to get rid of the irrelevant. Usually you will make a rough outline or at least list the major divisions you plan for your paper, but often you have to write a bit to find a pattern of organization. With a rough draft in hand, you can check to see that the structure holds together and make necessary revisions in your plan.

How Do I Present Myself and My Material?

Inevitably, the writer appears in the work. You are there.

Your voice and your approach or attitudes will be evident in what you put on paper.

The tone or attitude in your writing might do one of these:

- record—with varying degrees of objectivity and detachment.

- explain, justify—again, in varying degree.

- romanticize, sentimentalize—another way to look at the past or at a topic. (This tone is nostalgic—looking through rose-colored glasses.)

- laugh at/laugh with—the humor can vary from the satiric, fun-poking attitude to the light. Some of the best writing is done with a tone of once-over-lightly.

- praise, glorify—the two differ, even though both see greatness in the subject.

- interpret, analyze—the writer clarifies, shows why and how, offers insights or perspectives.

- regret, deplore—the writer is perhaps grieved over a situation, the past, an event, etc.

From thinking about these approaches, you can see how the writer's attitude will control selection of details and choice of language—what to put in, what to leave out, and how to say it.

If you are writing history or memoirs especially, you may also want to ask yourself, "What do I do about missteps and family skeletons?" Certainly, you don't want to whitewash, to be sentimental or unrealistic. You'll want to present persons who are fallible as well as those who are lovable; you'll want to admit errors as well as announce successes. So if no one will be hurt by the telling, and if the inclusion will enhance what you write, include the bad as well as the good, the warts as well as the dimples.

How Do I Achieve an Effective Style?

Your style is *you*. Not only is style individual, but you adapt your personal style to specific occasions, to the purpose and audience for which you are writing. Even though you choose a particular style to carry the tone that you wish to convey, there are some general precepts—some goals or characteristics— that mark an effective style.

Critics generally praise writers for styles that are clear, economical, appropriate, and emphatic. They also look for freshness of expression, the earmarks of individuality, so that a piece of writing is characterized by a distinct voice. While to some extent style is natural, achieving such effectiveness in writing is determined in part by how hard you work at it—by your choice of language, structure of sentences, selection and arrangement of detail, and way of ordering the parts to organize the whole.

Language

Writers are "word people." Words are your tools. The more you have at your command, the more effective your style. Consider these as goals:

- Language should be *varied*—variety comes from richness of vocabulary; saying things differently adds to interest and makes writing colorful.

- Language should be *exact*—exactness implies choosing words right for your purpose, naming things precisely, creating pictures with vivid details.

- Language should be *natural*—words should be chosen to express, not impress. The overly-elegant like the grotesque or coarse in language is almost always offensive, calling attention to the words rather than the meaning.

Sentences

Like the words you use, sentences need to be clear, varied, and emphatic. These goals imply the right connections (every part related clearly to others); variation in the patterns (short-long; simple-complex-compound; changing word orders), and sharp, terse, even dramatic arrangements (the main idea in the best position).

- Clarity requires right connections.

  —Modifying words and phrases should be placed as near as possible to words they modify ("For sale: Steinway piano by family moving with carved legs" just doesn't make sense! "Walking up the hill, the sunset was ahead" has the sunset taking a hike! "Only the union leaders wanted a short vacation"— try putting *only* in other places and see what happens to meaning.)

  —Connectives should make the right links between words and phrases. (Distinguish between *in* and *on, among* and *between, to* and *at*, etc.)

- Variety means that all sentences are not constructed on the same pattern. Lack of variety produces monotony.

  —Try sentences on the ear by reading your prose aloud ("While he went to town, she stayed home and prepared a very good company dinner," rather than "He went to town. She stayed home and prepared dinner. The dinner was for company. It was very good.")

  —Change patterns by placing a phrase at the first of the sentence to vary the common subject-verb order ("Slowly and sleepily, without looking at the dog, the cat stretched out on the hearth." Now start with "the cat"—the common order.)

• Emphasis comes from placing words and phrases in the best position.

—As with variety, emphasis goes hand-in-hand with the unexpected order. (Tennyson wrote "Into the valley of Death/Rode the six hundred," not "The six hundred rode into the valley of Death.")

—Fragments (incomplete sentences) are often emphatic and they are quite acceptable when they are clear. ("Wonder of wonders! Splendor of splendors! What a joy!" Such "detached parts" are frequently exclamations, but they need not be. Recall Had Manske's essay on nature poems: "It's a world of its own. With its own change and swing. Its own light and dark." With some purposes and contexts, fragments are appropriate.)

How Do I Edit My Work?

Of course, everyone likes to be "correct." Just as we once read Emily Post and our grandchildren now read Miss Manners, we are all more or less conscious of the need to clear up and clean up what we write. Being "more or less conscious," though, should not mean that you let accepted practices and rules make you hesitate to write. Here are a few useful guidelines to apply at the finish rather than along the way, where they might inhibit the flow of your thoughts. For more complete guides to conventions, buy any good handbook or locate one in your library.

How Can I Check the Punctuation?

Sumner Cotzin's review of punctuation appeared in *The Comp Post* published by the writing laboratory at Assumption College in Massachusetts. He calls this an "Easy Guide to Rules of Punctuation"—

To make a separation from a
Phrase or clause, employ a ,   Comma ,

To add an afterthought
   with ease,
It's wise to use ( )   Parentheses ( )

At ends of lines, it
   saves your life when
You split a long word with a -   Hyphen -

When quoting other
   lingual sharks,   Quotation
Be honest. Use " "   Marks " "

To ask the reader's eyes
   to whisk
To footnote, use an *   Asterisk *

Link two ideas which
   can't be stolen
Each from each by ;   Semicolon ;

To warn of an impending
   crash,
Precede your statement
   with a —   Dash —

Complete connection, on the
   whole, in
Two ideas requires a :   Colon :

A query—made when in
   the dark—   Question
Should finish with a ?   mark ?

For segregating sentences
   myriad
Each one is ended with a .   Period .

Words like "lo," "alas,"
     and "hark"   *Exclamation*
Require an !   *mark !*

* * *

When all balled up with rules, just tell
The silly things to, ( )-" " * ' ; —: ? . !

How Can I Check My Spelling?

Modernists are lucky—they can check their spelling with a computer program. However your state of the art may still be your well-worn dictionary. The time to check is, of course, as you proofread the nearly final copy. A warning: read for common words easily confused (*there, their*, etc.) and for those words that electronic mechanisms do not detect because the "misspelling" is still a "real" word. These are the spots where errors creep in undetected. Spelling programs are not smart enough to recognize the difference when a sentence that should read "He threw his *boot* across the room" appears as "He threw his *foot* across the room." In other words, you have to read for sense as well as spelling errors.

How Do I Check for Grammatical Conventions?

Actually, the trouble spots are few.

1. Like little birds in their nests, verbs are supposed to agree with antecedents: "Every *one* of the national holidays falls on a three-day weekend." Determine the subject. Be cautious of intervening words.

2. Pronouns not only must agree with antecedents ("When a nation faces crisis, *its* citizens are usually loyal" not "*their* citizens"), but must refer clearly to an antecedent: "She took a handkerchief out of her purse, blew her nose, and then put it in her pocket" may cause your reader to laugh. Be especially careful of vague reference for words like "which."

3. Distinguish between troublesome verbs (*lie, lay*) and the cases of pronouns (*I, me; he, him; they, them;* etc.).

4. Keep verb tenses consistent and in logical sequence. You can choose freely to set things back (past tense) or keep them in present, but the relationships should be clear.

How Do I Check for Economy?

Often we don't trust ourselves as writers. Unsure that our readers will get the point, we say a thing twice, or thrice.

1. Check for needless "repetition, redundancy, restatement, words saying the same thing." Now you can play with that one! Sometimes you purposely try several words, weigh them, and cut.

2. Watch out for traps in sentences beginning with words like *there* and *it*. These can be wordy and confusing: "There is a great deal of work and expenditure of tax money involved in the planning, laying out and keeping up of the new bicycle paths in our area." Or—"Building and maintaining local bicycle paths requires planning, city funds, and labor."

How Do I Proofread My Work?

You will proofread for all of these elements—the organization, the language, the conventions. A few hints can help you check your manuscript thoroughly and efficiently.

1. Let your writing rest for an hour, a day, whatever. Come back to it later.

2. Read slowly, line by line, using a ruler or sheet of paper to isolate each line.

3. Have someone unfamiliar with the material read the paper for you or with you.

4. Read into a tape recorder and listen to how your writing sounds *without* looking at the print.

5. Read backwards, bottom up, avoiding the trap of familiarity.

6. For special documents, follow the method of professionals, and read aloud (indicating all punctuation marks, paragraphing, etc.) to another person holding copy.

How Will I Package My Writing?

The form your published piece will take depends on—

how you plan for distribution
what audience you will reach
how much you have to spend
what you want as a final form

You have some alternatives. First, if you package for yourself and sharing with family and friends—

1. Write in longhand in a notebook. This form is simple, economical, and personal. If you want extra copies, duplicate inexpensively at a copy center.

2. Type copy or have it typed and duplicated; use a microcomputer and duplicate with the printer. Fasten pages into ring notebooks or snap binders, or even spiral binders.

3. Have your writing printed privately at your own expense, as did some of the writers we have quoted. You will need to get bids from more than one printer, and make decisions about the number and size of copies, and the special features such as graphics, pictures, covers, weight of paper.

   Be wary of advertisements and promises of subsidy printers, also called "vanity presses." The cost is usually high and the services minimal.

If you plan to submit your work to a publishing outlet—

1. Type or word process/print copy, double-spaced.

2. Use fresh black ribbon, good quality paper (not erasable type, which smudges).

3. Leave generous margins: at least one inch on each side, two inches from the top, one inch from the bottom.

4. Place name and address on top page, last name and page number on succeeding pages.

5. Proofread carefully.

6. Clip pages together; don't staple.

7. Send original; enclose SASE (self-addressed stamped envelope).

8. Keep a copy, *always*.

A Note: Sometimes you will want to sound out a prospective outlet by sending a *query letter*. Tell what you are writing, the approach you are taking, and the approximate length. Tell why you are qualified to handle the assignment and why you think the readers of the periodical or newspaper will appreciate what you offer them. Before you query, study the magazine or newspaper to know how your article might meet its needs.

Should I Take a Writing Course?

It is not essential to study writing formally in order to write. But there can be value in a writing group or writing course. Check out what is offered through extension courses, Elderhostels, etc. Talk to those who have participated in the past. Be wary of high cost, mail order, slick promotional deals. Look for a course

that provides opportunities to write,
that is organized as a community of writers,
that is led by an instructor who also enjoys writing.

And in a course or alone, find pleasure and help in this book.

Acknowledgments

(continued from copyright page)

"Quick Starts" printed by permission of Richard Behm.
Letter from Earl Proulx, editor "Plain Talk" column, *Yankee Magazine*, Dublin, New Hampshire, reprinted by permission of Mr. Proulx and *Yankee Magazine*.
News item from *The Manchester Press*, Manchester, Iowa, reprinted by permission.

CHAPTER 3

"It's Just One Darn Thing After Another" by Andy Rooney, 1985. Reprinted by permission: Tribune Media Services.
From *The Other Side of Silence: A Guide to Christian Meditation* by Morton P. Kelsey. Copyright © 1975 by The Missionary Society of St. Paul the Apostle. Used by permission of Paulist Press.
"Swapping Detergents, and Other Mistakes You Won't Repeat" by Sheila Taylor, *Bremerton Sun*, April 21, 1988. Reprinted by permission of Scripps Howard News Service.
"Partly Cloudy" from The Talk of the Town. Reprinted by permission; © 1984, *The New Yorker Magazine*, Inc.

CHAPTER 4

From " 'I Think (and Write in a Journal), Therefore I Am' " by Joseph Reynolds, from *The Christian Science Monitor*, February 23, 1981. Reprinted by permission of *The Christian Science Monitor*.
From "Self-Help: Journals and the Life Examined" by Carol Krucoff. Copyright © *The Washington Post*. Reprinted by permission.
From "Keeping a Journal" by Dorothy Lambert, *The English Journal*, February 1967. Copyright © by the National Council of Teachers of English. Reprinted with permission.
From *The Other Side of Silence: A Guide to Christian Meditation* by Morton P. Kelsey. Copyright © 1975 by the Missionary Society of St. Paul the Apostle. Used by permission of Paulist Press.
Excerpts from *Hal Borland's Book of Days* by Hal Borland. Copyright © 1976 by Hal Borland. Reprinted by permission of Alfred A. Knopf, Inc.
Selections from *The Country Diary of an Edwardian Lady* by Edith Holden. Copyright © 1977, Webb and Bower, Ltd. Reprinted by permission of Henry Holt and Company.
"Looking Back" by Edgar Harrison, from *Good Old Days*, October 1988. Copyright © The House of White Birches, Inc. Reprinted with permission.

CHAPTER 5

"The Way I Read a Letter's This" by Emily Dickinson. (Version in public domain.)
"Letter to Mrs. Bixby" by Abraham Lincoln. From *A Treasury of the World's Great Letters*, edited by M. Lincoln Schuster. Copyright © 1940. Reproduced by permission from Simon and Schuster, Inc.
A Letter to Her Mother, December 25, 1854, by Louisa May Alcott. From *Louisa May Alcott, Her Life, Letters and Journals*, edited by Ednah D. Cheney, Roberts Brothers, Boston, 1889.
Two letters to subscribers of *National Lampoon*. Reprinted by permission of *National Lampoon*, Inc.

CHAPTER 6

"Back to the Basics—Again" by William F. Steuber. *Wisconsin Academy Review*, Vol. 25, no. 4 (September 1979). Reprinted by permission.
"Seems to Me" by Henry Butler. *American Way* (American Airlines Magazine), March 1985. Reprinted by permission of the author.

CHAPTER 7

From *Writing the Natural Way* by Gabriele Rico. Copyright © 1983 by Jeremy P. Tarcher. Reprinted by permission of Jeremy P. Tarcher, Inc. and St. Martin's Press.

CHAPTER 8

Excerpt from "Skeletons, Saints, and a Sense of Self" by William J. Hofmann. *Puget Soundings*, October/November 1984. Reprinted by permission of the author.
"Changing Generations" by Maude B. Rogers. *Puget Soundings*, June 1984. Reprinted by permission of the author.
From *The Store (phone 306)* by Jean Kanable Birkett and Marian Kanable, 1986. Reprinted by permission of Jean Birkett.

CHAPTER 9

"Sharing Is What Verne Macdonnell Enjoys Most" by Phoebe Smith. *Bainbridge Review*, October 9, 1985. Reprinted by permission of the author and the *Bainbridge Review*.
"Elwood Haynes," biographical sketch by Robert S. Woodbury, *Encyclopedia Americana*, Vol. 13, 1976 edition. Reprinted by permission of Grolier Incorporated.
From *Mary Boykin Chestnut, A Biography* by Elizabeth Muhlenfeld. Copyright © 1981 by Louisiana State University Press. Reprinted by permission.
"The Quintessential New Englander—Fannie Farmer" by Lisa Hammel. *Yankee Magazine*, September 1985. Reprinted by permission of the author.
"A Highway Heads for Fifty" by L. F. Willard. *Yankee Magazine*, November 1984. Reprinted by permission of *Yankee Magazine*.
History of the Captiva Chapel by the Sea, courtesy of the Chapel.

CHAPTER 10

"Definition of Poetry" by Lynn Z. Bloom, from *College Composition and Communication*, February 1974. Copyright © 1974 by the National Council of Teachers of English. Reprinted with permission.
"Byron vs. DiMaggio" by Peter Meinke, from *The Night Tram and the Golden Bird*, University of Pittsburgh Press, 1977. Copyright © Peter Meinke. Reprinted by permission of the author.
"Religion Class," by Marguerite Kelly from TYPOG, Volume 2 (Winter 1973). Reprinted by permission of Scott, Foresman and Company.
"Lucinda Matlock" by Edgar Lee Masters, from *The Spoon River Anthology*. Reprinted by permission of Leavy, Rosensweig & Hyman, for the estate of Edgar Lee Masters.
"Sand Tarts" by Emma S. Thornton, from *The Stone in My Pocket*, 1981. Reprinted by permission of the author.
"Recipe for Daily Living" by Sadie Carlson. Frontispiece for cookbook of the Methodist Church, Paton, Iowa, 1939.

"For an Eighty-Seventh Birthday" by Jessie Farnham. Reprinted by permission of Rose Wasserman, for the estate of Jessie Farnham.

"Footwork" by Benjamin Hochman, *Modern Maturity*, December 1986-January 1987. Reprinted by permission of the author.

"The Man He Killed" by Thomas Hardy. From *The Complete Poems of Thomas Hardy*, edited by James Gibson, Macmillan Company (New York) 1978.

CHAPTER 11

"Perpetual Care" by Hazel F. Briggs. First printed in *Wisconsin Academy Review*, Vol. 27, no. 2 (March 1981); later part of a collection, *I'll Tell You Tomorrow and Other Stories* (1983). Reprinted by permission of the author and the *Wisconsin Academy Review*.

CHAPTER 12

"From the Trenches" by Paul Chance, *Psychology Today*, March 1988. Reprinted with permission from *Psychology Today Magazine*. Copyright © 1988 (PT Partners, L. P.)

Excerpt from "Second Opinions" by John Hartl, *The Seattle Times—The Seattle Post-Intelligencer*, November 3, 1985. Reprinted by permission.

CONCLUSION

"Why Do I Write?" by the late Bob Travis. First appeared in *The Courier-Journal*, Palmyra, New York. Reprinted by permission of Edward R. Travis.

APPENDIX: HELPFUL HINTS

Quotation from Annie Dillard. Reprinted by permission of Harper & Row, Publishers, Inc.

"Easy Guide to Rules of Punctuation" by Sumner Cotzin. *The Comp Post*, Assumption College, Worcester, Massachusetts. Reprinted by permission of the author.

From *The Store (phone 306)* by Jean Kanable Birkett and Marian Kanable. Reprinted by permission of Jean Birkett.

UNPUBLISHED MATERIALS

Special appreciation is due the writers in our various writing workshops—to Ray Hager for his letter to Earl Proulx and for "By the Numbers"; to Marjorie F. Warner for her family Christmas letter and for "Grandfather Buys Another Car"; to Ella Morse for a set of three letters; to Herb Boyce for "An Essay on Memory"; to Murilla Weronke for "Dogs Who Have Owned Us," "A Grandfather Sampler," and "Leah Leaving at Age Seven"; to Had Manske for "Nature Poems—How Come?" To these and several others whom we have "given" names but who asked to remain anonymous, we give thanks for allowing us to use their work.

We thank, too, several writers of memoirs who have told us of their ventures or who called attention to others involved in similar tasks. Carolyn and Arnold Peterson, Phyllis Norem, and Jean Kanable Birkett were especially kind to share experiences.

We thank Kenneth Wachowiak of the Department of Fashion and Interior Design, University of Wisconsin-Stevens Point, for his assistance with the cover design.

We thank Florence Ekstrand of Welcome Press, Seattle, Washington, for assistance and encouragement.

And we thank The Chapel by the Sea on Captiva Island, Florida, for a joyful Sunday service and a beautiful example of concise history.